Emotional Abuse Recovery:

Healing Your Heart after Codependent and Emotionally Abusive Relationships

How to Handle Narcissists, Controlling, Manipulative, Toxic People and Take Your Life Back

Martha McDowell

Disclaimer Notice:

Please note the information contained within this document is for educational and entertainment purposes only. All effort has been executed to present accurate, up to date, and reliable, complete information. No warranties of any kind are declared or implied. Readers acknowledge that the author is not engaging in the rendering of legal, financial, medical or professional advice. The content within this book has been derived from various sources. Please consult a licensed professional before attempting any techniques outlined in this book.

By reading this document, the reader agrees that under no circumstances is the author responsible for any losses, direct or indirect, which are incurred as a result of the use of information contained within this document, including, but not limited to errors, omissions, or inaccuracies.

Table of Contents

Introduction

Abuse is no laughing matter. It comes in all shapes and forms, and it can be present in more than just romantically inclined relationships. Abuse can be found in any relationship you might find yourself a part of; it could be a romantic relationship or even a relationship with your closest friend. If you have picked this book up, there might be some signs in one of your relationships that has you worried. Maybe you are reading for a friend, and maybe you want to arm yourself with the knowledge that can help you navigate the sticky world of relationships.

Whatever your reason for picking this book up is, one thing is certain— you will put it down having learned all you need to understand the difference between a healthy relationship and one in which you are being abused. Sometimes it can be hard to face the reality that we are in an abusive situation, and making excuses for a person becomes second nature, but what happens when you lose yourself in the abuse?

There are many kinds of abuse that a person can experience, and it can be hard to figure out if the situation you are in falls under abuse. Many people think that because they are not being physically touched or hit, they cannot call their experiences abuse.

Emotional abuse is a serious issue that many people go through and do not speak about because they do not think what they are experiencing is severe. The goal of this book is to introduce you to the different kinds of emotional abuse that you can experience in a relationship. While reading, you will discover what emotional abuse is, how to spot it in a relationship, and what to do about it once you know.

Read on to find out more about emotional abuse and how it can negatively affect you. Learn how to make a difference in the way you handle your relationships.

Chapter One: Types of Emotional Abuse

Abusive behavior can be hard to define or prove. There are many kinds of abusive behaviors, and these fall under six larger umbrella terms that define them. You might only be familiar with one or two, but through the course of this book you will learn to interpret the signs of the other types of abuse, too.

Physical abuse has the spotlight when it comes to abusive situations. People who experience physical abuse are often in perilous situations and isolated from areas of help. They might not even recognize their partner's behaviors as abusive. Abuse can come in any order, and sometimes physical abuse can be foreshadowed by other abuse types, such as emotional or verbal abuse. Other times, physical abuse is the precursor to the other abusive behaviors.

There is no set formula for how abuse happens and why, but there are a list of behaviors and attitudes to watch out for and examine in your relationship to ensure your safety.

So, what happens if the person you are in a relationship with has never hit you? That does not necessarily mean that you are in an abuse-free situation. Abuse comes in forms that are not limited to the physical.

To break down and understand what an abusive situation is or looks like, you need to understand what the abuse is and how to change the situation.

This is not another one of those books that just tells you about abuse. Through your journey, I seek to illustrate what abuse types look like and how to accurately depict if you are in an abusive situation. It is an interactive model that will help you get out if you need it. The key element is to remember that not all abuse is physical, so just because you might not have bruises on the outside does not mean you are not experiencing internal bruising.

The various types of abuse range from physical abuse, emotional abuse, verbal abuse, sexual abuse, financial abuse, neglect, and there are still more! Abuse really varies in the forms in which it appears.

Physical Abuse

Physical abuse occurs when one person in a relationship threatens physical bodily harm or uses external force against another in order to intimidate or keep control of them. It is important to remember that physical abuse does not have to result in bruises or cuts to be considered abuse. The threat alone of physically harming another person can be classified as physical abuse.

This type of abuse can appear in many different forms. If you are concerned that either you or someone you know might be in a relationship dominated by physical abuse, have a look at the signs that indicate abuse is occurring. Physical abuse can happen when a person bites, slaps, chokes, kicks, punches, or pulls your hair.

Forbidding a person from eating food or being allowed to sleep is another direct example of physical abuse. While they are not laying a finger on you, they are using physical intimidation to get a result that does not benefit you. Physical abuse also includes causing pain with any sort of weapon, preventing someone from calling the police or getting help, and driving recklessly when in the same vehicle.

These are just a few examples of ways in which physical abuse can manifest itself. Keep in mind, there are always other signs in which physical abuse demonstrates itself.

Verbal Abuse

Verbal abuse is often overlooked as a form of abuse, but it can have lasting effects on a person. Verbal abuse can happen when body language and words are used to criticize or put down another person viciously.

The goal of a person perpetrating verbal abuse against another is to lower the victim's self-esteem and lead them to believe that they are not worthy of respect or love. It can also manifest itself as a derogatory way of telling someone they have no talent or abilities to accomplish their goals.

The reason verbal abuse is so damaging is because it is often not recognized as abuse, and when left unchecked for periods of times, it not only devalues the person being abused, but it can also cause them to miss opportunities in life they otherwise might have taken.

Sexual Abuse

Any sexual contact that is unwanted is sexual abuse. It can occur in any relationship in a variety of ways and is extremely damaging. Sexual abuse shows itself when an abuser forces someone to dress or act in a sexual way, manipulates them or forces them into doing or performing sexual acts, holds them down during sex, and even intentionally passes on a disease to them.

These are only a few of the many ways in which sexual abuse occurs. Sexual abuse can also include the coercion or manipulation into having sex, for example, if an abuser makes one feel like they owe them something or if they give them drugs to “get them ready” for sexual acts.

Sexual abuse that occurs within a long-term relationship is often hard to prove. Abusers of children and adults alike often threaten their victims with bodily harm if they tell anyone that they are being abused, and the cycle of abuse continues.

Forms of Abuse

There are still many other abuse types not highlighted that can fall under the same category or even in their own niche, but recognizing the signs in which abuse can manifest itself can help you detect the signals early on and find an escape route.

A few takeaways from this chapter include the following:

- Abuse can occur in more than just a physical sense.
- Abuse can be sexual, physical, verbal, and even mental.
- Any behavior that feels as if you are being forced or coerced into doing something you do not want to do can be abuse or a display of abusive tendencies.

- It is harder to define abuse until you know what abusive behavior looks like.

I gave a brief overview of some other common abusive types. The focus of this book, however, is abuse that is not often discussed but is extremely damaging to the psyche. This abuse contains elements of verbal abuse, and they are often combined under the same blanket term. In the next chapter, I will define and highlight the ways in which emotional abuse occurs. When a person understands what emotional abusive behavior is, they are better prepared to handle it when they experience it, and it is often easier for them to find their way out of the situation.

Chapter Two: Emotional Abuse

Emotional abuse has many of its own subcategories. Because verbal abuse causes psychological damage to a person, it is also often classified under emotional abuse. Emotional abuse can also be called psychological abuse or mental abuse due to its effects on a person.

Emotional abusers use a person's feelings in order to mess with the victim's head and get them to comply with their abuser's wishes. Similar to verbal abuse, emotional abuse is often not recognized in its early stages, so the long-term ramifications for victims are often severe. If victims are able to pick up on the early signs of emotional abuse, they are more likely to get help or to get out of the situation.

While it is critical to identify when emotional abuse is happening to you, there are some instances that are not classified as abuse. Since it is so hard to identify, knowing what scenarios do not fall under emotional abuse can also help separate abusive behaviors from non-abusive behaviors.

Some instances that are not a situation of emotional abuse are:

- When a partner breaks up with you,
- A simple disagreement or argument with a partner,
- If someone is hurt by your actions, or
- When someone occasionally yells to express their emotions.

The situations above are not considered to be emotionally abusive. When the behavior occurs in an excessive manner that begins to affect your self-perception, then it might be time to re-evaluate the relationship and its effect on you.

Definition of Emotional Abuse

Emotional abuse is regarded as any abusive behaviors that do not involve physical violence. This can include humiliation, manipulation, intimidation, and verbal assaults, whose aims are to eradicate a person's sense of self-worth, dignity, and identity. The long-term ramifications from emotional abuse are suicidal thoughts or behaviors, post-traumatic stress disorder (PTSD), depression, and anxiety.

Since emotional abuse is such a broad term, it can house a lot of abusive behaviors that damage and affect a victim's mental state.

Emotional abuse can be present without any physical abusive behaviors present; however, physical abuse is always accompanied by emotional abuse. The interesting part is that both the emotional abuse and the physical abuse cycles follow the same patterns. Once the victim realizes the behaviors, the abuser tends to adjust their behaviors temporarily or further guilt the victim into believing they were in error.

Some signs of emotionally abusive behavior can include:

- Constantly being told you cannot do anything right.
- Becoming extremely jealous when spending time away from their partner.

- Being discouraged to see seeing friends or family; being isolated.
- Being controlled, being told what to do, where to go and who to see.
- Being blamed for what the abuser makes them do.
- Being tricked into questioning everything you know by their partner. It slowly drives them crazy. It's also known as gaslighting.

There are so many more ways in which emotional abuse manifests itself, and these are only a few key behaviors that you can look for to identify emotional abuse.

Remember, it does not always seem apparent to you when you or someone you know is being emotionally abusive. We often make excuses for our loved ones in these situations, but the longer we remain in an abusive situation, the worse your mental health becomes.

Chapter summary

Keep in mind that emotional abuse can manifest

itself in a relationship in different ways. If you want a quick run through of the main points, here you go:

- Emotional abuse can have long-term mental side effects on a victim.
- These side effects can include depression and be as severe as development of PTSD (post-traumatic stress disorder).
- Victims often make excuses for their abuser's behaviors.
- If you are isolated from family and friends, this is a big sign that you are being emotionally abused.
- Emotional abuse is interchangeable with other terms, like psychological abuse and mental abuse.

Over the next few sections and chapters, I will go more in-depth about what to do if you encounter emotional abuse, how to find out if your relationship is emotionally abusive, and developing a roadmap out of your abusive situation.

Remember! Emotional abuse can occur in more

than just a romantic relationship. A parent-child relationship or even just a friendship can have signs of emotional abuse as well.

Chapter Three: Abusive Nature

Okay, so we have all been there. You have had a bad day, and you take it out on someone you should not. Maybe you yell a little too loudly, or maybe you say something you later wish you had not. Does this mean you are an emotional abuser?

There is a line between being human and being abusive. People have bad days and people have disagreements. This does not necessarily mean they are abusive; so how do you tell then if your partner is just having a bad day or if they are emotionally abusing you?

Keep track of behavior patterns. Ask yourself after interactions with your partner, "How did that make me feel?" When a set of behaviors become a consistent pattern, it goes from a bad day to abusive. A disagreement with your partner does not necessarily constitute emotional abuse, and if your feelings get hurt from something they said, it might just be a bad moment for them.

Emotional abuse is a very serious abusive behavior that often gets swept under the rug, or takes a backseat to physical abuse, so it is important to know the signals of emotional abuse and be able to differentiate between a bad day and abusive behavior. This way we are better prepared to handle each situation as it arises.

If your partner has a disagreement with you or yells at you after a bad day, they might regret it. If they are willing to be open and communicate about it, it's easier for you to find that line between abuse and a bad moment. Listen to what your partner says when they are discussing the argument. A key element of emotional abuse is that an abuser will try to make you feel bad or guilty for the argument; they will tell you it was your fault.

Take that as a red flag. A partner who has a bad day should be able to communicate when they have done something wrong without making you feel responsible for it. A good sign to look for is when they are blaming you for the abuse.

Let me stop for a moment and clarify. You are not to blame for the abuse. Yes, they might say this and make you feel like you are, but that is what an emotional abuser does, and they are good at what they do. So, if you find yourself in a situation where you are being blamed for the abusive behavior done to you and you find yourself believing that you were the one at fault, take a step back. Analyze the situation and your emotions. When you do this, you might find you notice other key behaviors of theirs that indicate you are the victim of an emotional abuser.

Gaslighting

I want to take a moment and draw attention to a very common tactic that emotional abusers use: gaslighting. Maybe you've heard the term used before but are not sure what it means. It is commonly used by emotional abusers to skew your perception of reality.

Gaslighting is the practice of psychologically manipulating a person until they begin to question and doubt their own sanity. Since abuse is about control and power in a relationship, gaslighting is an extremely effective method of accomplishing this as it makes a victim question their sanity, their own feelings, and their gut instincts. The reason gaslighting is such a serious issue is because, once an abuser gets the victim to a point where they question themselves so intensely, a victim is less likely to leave the abuser or the abusive situation.

There are a few techniques involved when an abuser uses gaslighting that are important to look out for.

Withholding is one of those techniques. Withholding is where an abuser can pretend not to understand what a victim is saying, or even refuses to listen to them. They will indicate that the victim is trying to confuse them or is not making sense.

When an abuser questions a victim's memory of events, despite the fact that the victim remembers things correctly, they are using a technique called countering. This makes a victim question their memory and, in turn, their level of sanity.

Blocking and diverting are other key ways abusers use gaslighting on a victim. The abuser will either change the subject or question the victim's thoughts to cause internal conflict within the victim.

Have you ever heard someone tell you that you

are too sensitive or that you get angry or emotional for no reason? When a partner is using the technique called trivializing, they make the victim's needs seem unimportant or inconsequential.

The last behavior to look for to know if you are being gaslighted is the forgetting and denial technique. Here, an abuser will pretend to forget events or conversations that have transpired and deny things that they may have said or promised to the victim.

Sounds crazy right? All these techniques are used when an abuser is trying to gaslight a victim. This is why it is important to analyze how you are feeling after interactions with your partner, and it is also important to understand what emotional abuse looks like so you can stop it before you become a victim.

Gaslighting does not happen overnight. It occurs slowly over time in a relationship. An incident or two may seem harmless to the victim, but, over time, they will lose their sense of self, become anxious and depressed, and even feel isolated. Once the victim enters into these feelings, they begin to rely more on their abusive partner. This makes it a harder situation to escape.

If you are wanting to analyze your feelings to see if you are being gaslighted, here are some common signs victims of gaslighting experience:

- You are always second-guessing yourself;
- You do not think you are good enough to be with your partner;
- It seems like you cannot do anything right;
- You may feel confused, and even crazy;
- You are always the one to apologize to your partner;
- You remember your former self as a different person;
- You excuse your partner's behaviors not only to yourself but to your friends and family;
- You feel/know something is wrong, but you cannot express it;
- You have trouble making simple choices; or
- You hide information to avoid put-downs or feelings of confusion brought on by

your partner.

The above signs are a few of the most common feelings victims of gaslighting have reported to experience. If, while reading this, you feel like you can identify with these feelings, take a moment to step back and evaluate the status of your relationship. If you need help, go and speak to someone besides your partner that you can trust for advice. If you are unsure about whom you can or cannot trust, reach out for help at the National Domestic Violence Hotline by calling or even live chatting with them if you do not want to call.

Chapter summary

A few important takeaways from this chapter are:

- Not all moments of anger or disagreement are abuse.
- There is a line between being human and being abusive.
- Constantly being blamed for arguments is an indicator you are being emotionally abused.

- Gaslighting is the main technique used by abusers.
- Gaslighting can cause a victim to lose a sense of themselves and their sanity.
- If you think you are being emotionally abused, reach out to the National Domestic Violence Hotline at 1-800-799-SAFE (7233) or 1-800-787-3224.

Now that you understand and can interpret the line between being human and being abusive, we will delve into some exercises and worksheets that might help you better determine whether you are in an abusive situation and what to do about it.

Chapter Four: How to know if you are Emotionally Abused

Even with all the outlines and information given, sometimes it is still hard to depict whether we are being emotionally abused or not. If we are, it can be easy to make excuses for our own situations because the lines are blurred, but what happens when someone else is experiencing your same situation?

Case studies are an in-depth analysis of a situation, and they can help you see what an emotionally abusive situation looks like for someone that is experiencing it. If you identify with the situation and you feel outraged, scared, or sadness for the people mentioned in the case study, you might want to analyze your own relationship to see if you might be excusing the same behaviors.

Olga's Issue

Olga says that if her abuser had punched her in the face the first time they had gone out, then she would never have gone back, but the truth of what he did was so much worse. They got married after a 9-month whirlwind romance. She was in an emotionally vulnerable place, and he made her feel secure.

At first, his jealousy was endearing to Olga. She would think it was cute that he cared that much about her. Slowly, his behavior went from subtle comments about her shoes or a skirt to telling her that people were going to be staring at her in her skimpy outfits, and eventually just telling her she dressed like a prostitute.

They had a daughter together that he did not parent very much. He made his wife quit her job so that she could take care of the home. When Olga went to fetch her daughter from school, she was timed. He would call the home to ensure that she got back in an appropriate amount of time from picking their daughter up.

Olga stayed at home, stopped seeing her friends and family, and took care of him. He would come home to freshly ironed shirts and a clean house. Olga remarks on how he always wanted the shirt that was dirty, though. It did not matter how many shirts she ironed, it was always the wrong shirt.

Things really started to throw Olga off when he would not let her go to the doctor for check-ups. Olga's abuser told her that all she wanted was to get naked in front of a doctor. In an emergency, Olga wound up at the doctors and found out her ovaries had to be removed. His response to her was that she had done it to spite him.

Olga was stuck in the relationship for seven years, and she believes that if she had stayed in longer, the relationship would have killed her. He threatened to kill her, in the end.

Olga says that even after three years, she still goes to therapy. She believed she was worthless and her identity was gone and vanished. She remarks that she was a happy person before him, an outgoing person.

The Point in Olga's Story

Olga's story highlights several techniques of emotional abuse. Her abuser uses guilt to make her feel as if everything is her fault. In the previous chapters, I have highlighted the emotions that are felt by victims of emotional abuse, and Olga depicts those in her emotional story as well.

Olga was able to get herself help when she saw the effect the abuse was having on her own child, and it was becoming harder to deny his effect on her child. She was disorientated about what her abuser was doing to her.

He used gaslighting techniques to confuse Olga and make her believe that there was nothing she could do correctly. Olga ended up relying on her abuser for support, without realizing he was causing her to feel the way she was.

While this particular case study does depict the abuser as male, men are not the only perpetrators of emotional abuse, and there are also many cases where women have been emotionally abusive to men. Whether it is a male or female perpetrating the abuse, the results are the same for the victim. Getting out of an abusive situation as soon as possible is the best thing for your mental health.

If you identify with any part of Olga's story or emotions, keep reading. There is still a lot more to cover and explore about being in an emotionally abusive situation.

Emotional Abuse Quiz

Below, there will be a brief quiz. It is easy to continue to make excuses for our partners; it becomes a little harder when the answers are staring us right back in the face. Throughout this book, we will do a few exercises that can help you navigate whether or not you are being emotionally abused. This quiz can be taken with a romantic partner in mind, or you can assess a non-romantic relationship you might have doubts about.

Do you:

- ✓ Feel afraid of your partner most of the time?

- Yes
- No
- At times

✓ Avoid certain topics out of fear of angering them?

- Yes
- No
- At times

✓ Feel like you cannot do anything right for them?

- Yes
- No
- At times

✓ Believe that you deserve to be mistreated or hurt?

- Yes
- No
- At times

- ✓ Wonder if you are crazy?
    - o Yes
    - o No
    - o At times
- ✓ Feel emotionally numb or helpless?
    - o Yes
    - o No
    - o At times

Do they:

- ✓ Humiliate or yell at you?
    - o Yes
    - o No
    - o At times
- ✓ Criticize and put you down?
    - o Yes
    - o No
    - o At times

- ✓ Make you embarrassed to see family and friends?
    - o Yes
    - o No
    - o At times
- ✓ Put down/ignore your accomplishments?
    - o Yes
    - o No
    - o At times
- ✓ Blame you for their abusive behavior?
    - o Yes
    - o No
    - o At times
- ✓ See you as their property?
    - o Yes
    - o No
    - o At times
- ✓ Have an unpredictable temper?

- Yes
- No
- At times

✓ Threaten to hurt or kill you?

- Yes
- No
- At times

✓ Threaten to take your children away?

- Yes
- No
- At times

✓ Threaten to commit suicide if you leave?

- Yes
- No
- At times

✓ Force you to have sex when you do not want to?

- Yes

- No
- At times

✓ Act jealous and possessive to limit who you see?

- Yes
- No
- At times

✓ Control where you go or what you do?

- Yes
- No
- At times

✓ Isolate you from friends and family?

- Yes
- No
- At times

✓ Limit your access to money and transport?

- Yes
- No

- At times

- ✓ Constantly check up on you?
    - Yes
    - No
    - At times

Fill in the circle if you feel like your partner is exhibiting any of these behaviors towards you and calculate how many questions you said yes to.

The more questions that you answered yes to, the more likely you are to be in an abusive situation. If you answered yes to most of the questions, the odds are you already know you are being emotionally abused but are unsure about how to get out of it. That is okay; this is why you are reading this book. We will help you find a way to plan your way out from the situation safely.

Self-Worth

Even after taking the previous quiz, you might still have some doubts. Emotional abuse is a very serious problem that often goes undetected for a long period of time. There are direct correlations between emotional abuse and a person's level of self-worth, anxiety, and depression.

Below, take the test to see where your self-worth lies.

1. I generally feel pretty good about myself as a person.
    - Strongly Disagree – 1
    - Disagree Somewhat – 2
    - Neutral – 3
    - Agree Somewhat – 4
    - Strongly Agree – 5
2. Most people I know are more intelligent and capable than I am.
    - Strongly Disagree – 1

- Disagree Somewhat – 2
- Neutral – 3
- Agree Somewhat – 4
- Strongly Agree – 5

3. Most people I know are more attractive than I am.
    - Strongly Disagree – 1
    - Disagree Somewhat – 2
    - Neutral – 3
    - Agree Somewhat – 4
    - Strongly Agree – 5
4. Most people I know are more interesting than I am.
    - Strongly Disagree – 1
    - Disagree Somewhat – 2
    - Neutral – 3
    - Agree Somewhat – 4
    - Strongly Agree – 5

5. I am often surprised to find out that other people see me more positively than I see myself.

    - Strongly Disagree – 1
    - Disagree Somewhat – 2
    - Neutral – 3
    - Agree Somewhat – 4
    - Strongly Agree – 5

6. I feel like I am a pretty good catch as a relationship partner.

    - Strongly Disagree – 1
    - Disagree Somewhat – 2
    - Neutral – 3
    - Agree Somewhat – 4
    - Strongly Agree – 5

7. When I complete a challenging task, it makes me feel good about myself.

    - Strongly Disagree – 1
    - Disagree Somewhat – 2

- Neutral – 3
- Agree Somewhat – 4
- Strongly Agree – 5

8. How I feel about myself is determined to a large extent by what others think about me.
    - Strongly Disagree – 1
    - Disagree Somewhat – 2
    - Neutral – 3
    - Agree Somewhat – 4
    - Strongly Agree – 5

9. I often find myself thinking negative thoughts about myself.
    - Strongly Disagree – 1
    - Disagree Somewhat – 2
    - Neutral – 3
    - Agree Somewhat – 4
    - Strongly Agree – 5

10. I often have a hard time understanding why someone would be interested in me romantically or sexually.

   - Strongly Disagree – 1
   - Disagree Somewhat – 2
   - Neutral – 3
   - Agree Somewhat – 4
   - Strongly Agree – 5

Now that the test is done, add together the total your answers scored. For example, the answers to questions 1 through 10 each have a number ranging from one to five. Add up your answer from each question to find out where you fall on the scale of self-worth.

If you scored between:

10-25: you seem to have a low sense of self-worth. Poor self-worth can get in the way of you accomplishing your goals and dreams. It can also make it more challenging to lead a healthy romantic relationship. This can indicate that your ideas about yourself are wrong.

26-40: You have a moderate sense of self-worth.

You have some negative feelings about yourself that could be improved. Keep in mind that you do not always have to be so harsh with yourself. Think about why you think about yourself in a negative light at times.

41-50: Congrats! Your feelings of self-worth are spot on. Having a good self-worth can positively impact your romantic relationships and your ability to conquer your aspirations.

If you scored low on this test, you might want to evaluate why these feelings of low self-worth plague you. It could be because of the emotional abuse that you have received from your partner. Be honest with yourself when taking these tests.

If you scored low on this test but on the previous quiz you answered that you were not emotionally abused, go up and take it one more time. Open up and be honest about how your partner makes you feel.

Relationships are riddled with insecurities. There are so many factors in a relationship that can cause a person to doubt themselves. The one thing you do not want to do is accuse a partner of being emotionally abusive if you are not sure.

That is the purpose of this book, to help you

navigate this sticky situation and point you in the right direction for help and resources.

Right now, you might be freaking out inside because the quiz revealed that your partnership might be emotionally abusive. Relax. I will take you through the steps and information you need to know to prepare yourself. It will not be easy, but hey! You have made it this far, and you've got a few more steps in you.

Let us take some time and go over some common misconceptions when it comes to abusive situations.

Many people believe that abuse does not happen to those in high school, college, or the generally educated population. This is a false notion. Abuse can happen in any relationship regardless of gender, race, age, or educational level.

Also, it can be common to believe that once a person leaves an abusive situation, that the abuse ends. This is usually the time when a victim is most at risk. Experts recommend safety planning for the victim, as the abuser can be volatile during a separation.

Sometimes friends have the best intentions but conduct them in the worst of ways. Some people believe that the best way to get a loved one to leave an abusive situation is to cut their ties with the victim. This is one of the worst things you can do to help a friend in an abusive situation. Because an abuser's main goal is to have their victim rely on only them, you are further isolating a friend if you cut ties with them. A victim needs support from friends and family in order to find their way out.

If you are a friend and you are reading this book to find out how to help someone, keep reading. Understanding their situation will give you more insight into how to help them. They might not be willing to listen to what you have to say about their relationship, but, if you are armed and ready with the knowledge needed to help, you can provide more support when they need it most.

You could be the abuser

So, maybe you took the quiz above, and you did not identify with any of the situations. Maybe there is a nagging thought at the back of your head that you portray some of these traits towards your partner. Are you abusive?

Remember that physical abuse does not always occur in situations where there is emotional abuse. Often, there are times when the perpetrators are unaware that they are being emotionally abusive toward their partners.

They may be aware of their feelings of insecurity and jealousy about their partner but not know how to process it. The abuser might believe that they know what is best for their partner and, in turn, tries to control what they eat, to where they go, and how they dress. While some abusers know exactly what they are doing, it does occur that emotional abuse displayed stems from the abuser's own feelings of inadequacy or lack of control.

If the question is still nagging at you, there is a short quiz you can take to find out if you are guilty of showing abusive behavior towards your partner.

Do you:

- ✓ Make them afraid in order to control their behavior?
    - o Yes
    - o No

- At times

✓ Stop them from talking about things that upset you?

- Yes
- No
- At times

✓ Make them check everything with you first because they cannot be trusted?

- Yes
- No
- At times

✓ Verbally hurt them to keep control?

- Yes
- No
- At times

✓ Make them think they are crazy when they defy you?

- Yes

- No
- At times

✓ Play games and deny what you have said or act as if you were joking if they get upset about something you say?

- Yes
- No
- At times

✓ Believe that you are the one with the right to make up all the rules?

- Yes
- No
- At times

✓ Yell at or humiliate them if they annoy you?

- Yes
- No
- At times

✓ Criticize them to keep them in place?

- Yes
- No
- At times

✓ Isolate them from spending time with other people?

- Yes
- No
- At times

✓ Ignore or put down their accomplishments?

- Yes
- No
- At times

✓ Tell them it is their fault if you get angry or abuse them?

- Yes
- No
- At times

- ✓ Believe that they belong to you and should do as you say?
    - o Yes
    - o No
    - o At times
- ✓ Have a bad and unpredictable temper?
    - o Yes
    - o No
    - o At times
- ✓ Threaten to hurt them if they push you too far?
    - o Yes
    - o No
    - o At times
- ✓ Threaten to take their children away if they try to leave you?
    - o Yes
    - o No

- At times

✓ Threaten to commit suicide if they leave?

- Yes
- No
- At times

✓ Have sex with them even if they do not want to?

- Yes
- No
- At times

✓ Feel jealous and possessive over them?

- Yes
- No
- At times

✓ Control what they do and where they go?

- Yes
- No
- At times

- ✓ Keep them from seeing friends and family?
  - o Yes
  - o No
  - o At times
- ✓ Make them give you receipts and change back when you give them money?
  - o Yes
  - o No
  - o At times
- ✓ Track them electronically, or check up on them constantly?
  - o Yes
  - o No
  - o At times
- ✓ Read their mail, texts or emails without their knowledge?
  - o Yes
  - o No

- At times

The more answers you have answered yes to, the higher the likelihood that you are being emotionally abusive. All these questions signal behaviors that indicate emotional abuse is taking place.

If you answered yes to most of the above questions, then you might have been told you are abusive or are aware that you are. There are resources to assist you as well if you want to change your ways and learn how to be in a healthy relationship. Do not resist counseling. Counseling can be a wonderful benefit to help someone out who is an emotional abuser and help them resolve the feelings that cause them to manipulate others.

What do you do if you are in a relationship but still want to stay together? It is vital that both the abuser and the victim go through counseling and therapy separately. As emotional abuse has long-term ramifications on a victim, if you are aware of your behaviors, take immediate action for both you and your partner. Allow your partner to complete therapy and make their own decisions. If you both decide to move forward, the next step will be couples' therapy together.

Chapter summary

Wow! What a lot of information. Here are a few highlights:

- If you are being abused, there is always help. There is a way out.
- If you are the abuser, there is help too! Be proactive and seek out help for yourself.
- Abuse can happen to anyone; it does not happen only within a certain group.
- The most dangerous time for a victim is when they get ready to leave their abuser.

Change is possible, both if you are the victim or the abuser. As a victim, you can find your way out and back to yourself again. As an abuser, you can find help for yourself and locate from where you need to control stems. Some people stay together despite a situation that involves abuse; some people stay apart.

The important thing to know is that, if you are being abused, you need to get out and get some help. You cannot save your partner, and it is not your job to secure their emotional security because you need to work on your own. You lose yourself when you are in an emotionally abusive relationship, and the first person you need to help is yourself.

Taking the quizzes might have taken a lot out of you. It can be hard to face the reality that someone we think we love has been manipulating us, so I will quickly recap this chapter to keep these ideas fresh in your mind.

- Olga's case study demonstrates how deeply emotional abuse can affect a person and/or family.
- Her case highlights the ways in which emotional abuse is perpetrated in everyday life.
- The quiz can help you identify whether your relationship is emotionally abusive.
- Emotional abuse can occur in any relationship, and it does not have to be romantically inclined.

I hope this chapter has helped you understand more about the ways in which emotional abuse crops up in our lives, and what this particular monster can look like. In the next few chapters, we are going to look at emotionally abusive situations in more depth.

Chapter Five: Difficulty in Assisting Abused People

"Olga" read a magazine article that finally helped her understand why her husband was so controlling. He took charge of everything, from what they ate, to what she did, and even how she dressed.

At first, Olga thought it was endearing that he put so much thought into her clothes and how she presented itself. She even liked that he ordered food for her when they went out, and she never minded cooking his favorite meals for him at home; she wanted him to be happy.

Olga did not like it when he suggested she quit her job, but, after he came home and yelled at her about how he never had the clean clothes he wanted to wear, she understood his point of view.

Maybe it had seemed odd before to Olga that she never saw her family anymore and that her friends had stopped coming around a while ago, but it never clicked until she saw that article about emotional abuse. Now she knew how to help her husband! She just had to get him to talk to her.

The problem with Olga's situation above is that often victims of emotional abuse do not understand the gravity of their situations. Olga cannot help her husband as long as she remains in an emotionally abusive environment.

A person that is an emotional abuser will not be open to any discussion that suggests they have been emotionally abusing you. More often than not, they will turn the situation around and make you feel guilty for doubting them in the first place. You will find yourself trapped in the cycle of emotional abuse all over again as you internalize your conflict over their abuse.

Sometimes the victim can even feel like they deserve the abuse. Let me be clear here: under no circumstances does a victim deserve the abuse they are receiving.

As a victim of emotional abuse, your primary concern should not be how to talk the problem out with your partner, but how to protect yourself. You need to be aware of the dangers of repeating the cycle of emotional abuse and finding yourself help to deal with the psychological damage the abuse has already done to you.

Remember that a victim of emotional abuse can have severe depression, anxiety, and even feel as if they are losing their sanity, so it is important you get yourself to a trusted place for help and therapy. There is no easy path or way to heal from emotional abuse.

The Cycle of Emotional Abuse

I know it may be hard to hear that you cannot help your abuser yourself. I know it might be even harder to hear that you need to put yourself first in this situation. There is no easy way out of abuse, and the reason it is so vital for you remove yourself as soon as you can is because this is a cycle. The longer you stay and try to help, the more you get pulled into the cycle and the harder it becomes for you to leave.

The emotional abuse cycle comes in six parts. It starts with abuse, where your partner lashes out at you using humiliating or belittling behavior. They do this in order to maintain control and demonstrate that they are in charge.

Guilt comes after the abuse. Normally, your abuser will feel guilt over their actions. It is vital that I clarify that your abuser will generally feel guilt over potentially being caught, not because of the abuse they have subjected you to.

Excuses will follow their feelings of guilt. They will rationalize to you their behaviors and even blame you for the reasons they abused you in the first place. They want to escape the responsibility of their actions.

For a brief moment, they will cycle through displays of normal behavior. In this phase, they will act as if nothing happened; they might even turn on extra charm to make the victim feel at ease. This lures the victim into a false sense of security.

After the phase of normal behavior passes, they enter into a fantasy period where they dream of regaining control over you again. Here they plan ways of punishing you for what they think you have done wrong.

Once the fantasy is over, they work to set up the scene where they can justify abusing you. After this, the abuse cycle starts over again. A victim can easily get re-trapped into this cycle once they find out their partner is emotionally abusing them. An abuser will make the victim feel like it is their fault and they deserve the treatment that they are receiving.

Breaking this cycle once you are aware of it will be important for your recovery and your psychological health. Emotional abuse is directly correlated with your psychological health; therefore, the more abuse you endure, the more work you will have to do to combat the feelings of depression, anxiety, and PTSD.

Emotional abuse can be a tough situation to work out. It is understandable that you might be hesitant or concerned about your relationship. No one wants to accuse their partner of emotional abuse, but no one should want to put themselves in jeopardy, either.

In a more direct black-and-white way, I have devised a list of signs you may be missing or ignoring in your relationship that can point to emotional abuse being present. They include:

- ✓ They make you feel scared.
- ✓ They dictate incessant lectures or painful comparisons to others.

- ✓ They claim that you are always at fault.
- ✓ They have possessive jealousy.
- ✓ They humiliate you and make big demands of you that they know you cannot fulfill.
- ✓ They isolate you.
- ✓ They make you dependent on them.
- ✓ They think for you.

These eight symptoms are direct indications that you are being emotionally abused. If you feel like even one of these is an aspect of your relationship, talk to someone. It can even be someone you don't know, like a help line. Sometimes saying it out loud to yourself can also make you realize the situation you are in.

Statistics on abuse are grim. According to the National Domestic Hotline, 24 people per minute are victims of some form of abuse. That is 24 people in sixty seconds! That means every 2.5 seconds there is a case of abuse being perpetrated against someone. That number leads to more than 12 million men and women as victims a year.

That number is staggering. These are the

numbers for people who are in intimate relationships.

Why do they stay, you ask? Well, they are the same reasons you might be questioning leaving your own relationship right now. People stay in abusive situations for a variety of reasons. Some of the most common involve fear. The fear of what will happen to them if they leave the relationship encourages them to stay.

There are those that are used to abuse and believe that this type of behavior is normal. Those that find themselves in this situation might not know what a healthy relationship looks like, and, since this is the behavior they are used to, they accept it.

A different dynamic in an LGBTQ (Lesbian, Gay, Bisexual, Questioning, and Transgender) relationships could be the fear of being "outed." This means that they may not have come out to their friends or family yet, and their abuser could be threatening to "out" them if they leave.

The effect of embarrassment and shame should not be underestimated in this situation. It is often hard or difficult for some people to face that they have been emotionally abused. This can stem from a fear of judgment from peers and family; they may even think they have done something wrong to end up in an abusive relationship and are embarrassed to say they made a mistake.

If you are in an emotionally abusive situation, you know the effect it can have on your self-esteem. Low self-esteem might be another reason a person stays in the cycle of abuse. When they are constantly put down by their partner, they might not believe that they deserve any better. They might think it is their fault that they are being treated this way. (If you feel this way, let me tell you, it is absolutely NOT your fault.)

Here comes the big one: love. Many victims feel love for their abusive partners. This is not a weird thing to feel. It is expected that, in an intimate romantic relationship, there would be feelings of love attached. This emotion can be heightened if those involved have children. Their thoughts, then, would mainly be to keep their families together.

When love is involved, the victim often remembers how charming their partner was in the beginning. The victim might want the abusive behaviors to stop but to keep the relationship going.

There are also cultural and religious reasons why people stay in abusive situations. Sometimes it seems like the better option to prevent bringing shame upon your family.

Immigration status can affect victims as well. If they are undocumented, they might worry that reporting or leaving the abusive situation could have an effect on their immigration status. Language barriers can be at play here, too. It might be hard for a person whose first language is not the main language spoken in a country to communicate their experiences to those that can help.

A lack of money and resources can also compel a person to stay with an emotionally abusive partner. This can also fall under the umbrella of financial abuse, particularly if a victim is financially dependent on their partner.

When a person who is disabled feels physically dependent on their partner, it can cause a big issue for them to leave the safety they find in their abuser.

These are the main reasons people cannot leave their partners. Most of them cite a dependency on their partner, or a fear of being outed by their partners. This is never an easy situation to handle, and it can be made even more complicated by children.

Keep in mind though that if you are suffering from emotional abuse, it does not mean your children are not. They could be just as harmed as you are.

Chapter summary

This chapter covered a lot about emotional abuse. Before we move on, let us recap a few points:

- It is not your job to help your abuser.
- You are not at fault for your abuser's behavior. You do not deserve to feel worthless.
- Emotional abuse, like other abuse types, works in a cycle.
- The cycle goes from abuse to guilt, to excuses, normal behavior, fantasy, set-up, and right back to abuse again.
- It can be hard for a victim to break themselves away from a cycle of abuse.

- There are major signs to look out for when you believe you might be suffering from emotional abuse.
- These signs can include being scared of your partner, put down by your partner, and even cruelly compared to others by your partner.
- People tend to stay in abusive relationships for an assortment of reasons; it is important to understand these and be conscious of them if you are trying to help a loved one out of an abusive situation.

In the next few chapters, we will explore safety planning and a roadmap to your way out of an abusive situation.

Chapter Six: Speaking About Emotional Abuse

It is natural to want to work things out with someone that you have dedicated time and energy to. For those who were initially unaware of the ways in which an emotional abuser treats their victims, by this point in the book, you should have a clearer idea. You should now be equipped with the tools to differentiate the line between being human and being abusive.

Some of you might still want to work things out with your partner despite their abusive behavior. Maybe they have not hit extremes yet, and you think there is still a way to save the relationship. Whatever your reasons are, they are valid, as long as you ensure that you get the help you need to process how the cycle of emotional abuse has affected you.

So, what do you do when you want to work on things? How do you approach discussing emotional abuse with your partner in a healthy way? What happens if you get stuck in the cycle when they blame you again?

Excellent questions! Well, in this next section, we discuss exactly how to approach these questions with your partner.

You might also be wondering if it is worth trying to save your relationship or talk it out with your partner. You might not know the answer to this initially. That is okay. I suggest talking with a professional. Get in touch with a therapist and talk to them about your feelings and concerns. They can help you work through your feelings about the relationship.

Another option, if you are unclear, is to talk to your partner and take some time away from each other. You might be able to make clear choices if you do not feel like you are tied to them or owe them an answer. Suggest that your partner talk to a therapist, too, and then try couples' therapy. There are many routes to go for those that are emotionally wavering on staying together as a couple.

While emotional abuse is an extremely distressing form of abuse for the human psyche, there are still levels to how badly the abuser is perpetrating these behaviors. Keep in mind that what works for you might not work for someone else. As humans, we all operate and think differently, so not every solution fits the situation. That is why open communication with your partner and honesty with yourself is so important.

The Occasional Abuser

Let me get this out of the way right now. If you did the quizzes, have read the book up until this point, and you still find yourself justifying your partner's abusive behavior, STOP. Abuse is abuse. An occasional abuser is still an abuser.

Bear in mind I am not talking about your partner having a bad human moment and yelling too loudly or saying something they probably regret later. I am talking about emotionally abusive behaviors that have been described in the course of this book, where you experience emotions such as fear, feelings of isolation, and even start to question your own self due to your partner's emotional abuse.

If your partner emotionally abuses you, but it

happens only occasionally, be aware that this is a misconception. Your partner's abuse cycle takes longer to cycle back to where you can feel the abuse happening to you. It does not mean that they are not abusing you and that you are okay.

Any amount of emotional abuse can cause feelings of depression and anxiety, so it is essential that you understand that your case and your feelings are still very real and very important, even if you only feel like the abuse occurs on an occasional basis.

If you want to work things out in a situation where you feel like you are occasionally abused, that is okay too; you need to understand what to expect going into a conversation with someone who might be defensive about their behaviors. Prepare yourself for the probability that your partner might blame you as well for their abusive behaviors. Read ahead to find some clues and tips on how to have such a sensitive conversation.

Talking

Talking to someone about their abusive behavior is never an easy task, especially if the person is adept at masking or concealing their behaviors.

You might find comfort in getting a journal and writing things down. Write down the ways in which they emotionally abuse you and how it affects you. If you think that your partner might be gaslighting you, a journal will be particularly helpful so that you can keep track of what was said and what was done in situations that your partner tries to twist.

Another option, in addition to the journal or without it, can be to have a neutral third party sit in on your conversation to be a mediator and supporter. This person should not incite an argument or fight but should know how to diffuse the situation. This person is normally called an emotional shield, as they act as a buffer between you and your emotional abuser.

These confrontations do not always refer to romantic partnerships. It could be a parent, child, sibling, or even a friend that you share a relationship with. Emotional abuse is not strictly reserved for intimate relationships and can happen in any relationship where two people are active participants.

While it may seem unconventional to most, another way to put a shield between you and your abuser is to conduct the conversation over the telephone. You always risk that they might end the call without completely hearing you out, but if there is not a third party you trust to act as an emotional shield, this is another solution.

Conducting such a sensitive conversation where you confront your abuser about their behaviors over the phone can be challenging, but it provides a safe space where they have to hear you out, and it makes it harder for them to emotionally manipulate you back into their cycle of abuse.

If you do have a person that you trust and use as an emotional shield during this very difficult conversation, consider having it in a public area. You can try a semi-public area where you can still have some privacy, but the person you are confronting is forced to keep their voice down and listen to what you have to say.

It is actually important that, as a victim, you decide where and how to confront your abuser if you choose to do so. The reason for this is because this is your first step in reclaiming your power in decision-making. This will be your first attempt at controlling an area and situation in your life.

If you have a friend that you are concerned about, approach the subject with them carefully. Be aware that they might not be receptive to your thoughts about their relationship. Respect what decision they make and aim to be their support. They might realize it on their own and, when they do, they will need you in their corner.

The most crucial part you can play is to be their support system when they realize what kind of situation they are in. By being there for them, you can ensure that their feelings of isolation are lessened, and it is more likely that they will come to you for help. Be patient and be there. Those are the two best things you can do as a friend to someone in an emotionally abusive situation.

Dealing with Your Realization

So, now you are at the point where you may have just realized that you are in an abusive situation. Maybe it has just dawned on you, or perhaps you have fully accepted the fact that your relationship is an unhealthy one.

That is a good start! The first step in solving any problem is identifying that there is one in the first place. If you can identify that you are being emotionally abused, you have taken solid steps towards fixing the problem. Keep in mind that there are levels of emotional abuse. Some abusers can penetrate deep into a victim's psyche and cause high levels of harm, while other abusive situations are milder and do not cross as many lines. Regardless of the level of abuse, emotional abuse should still be taken seriously, but the level of abuse you might experience from your partner can severely impact your willingness to continue or end the relationship.

Whether you choose to stay in the relationship, work on the relationship, or walk away is completely up to you. Some people decide that they have nothing more to say and they want to find their way out of the relationship and towards themselves again. Other people that decide to leave might still want to confront their abuser.

Once you deal with your realization, it really depends on you what your next step is. For those that want to leave immediately, chapter eight will have some great tips on creating a safety plan!

If you decide you want to confront your abuser, keep reading for some more tips and clues. Talking to them might make you feel better, or you might have hopes of working things out. That's great. If, for some reason you find that even after talking it out you are unable to continue a relationship with the person, then chapter eight will have some great information for you as well.

Steps to Confronting Your Abuser

The first step mentioned above is to see and recognize the cycle of abuse. After this is done, it can be cathartic to speak it out loud. Try and identify all the tactics of abuse that are being used against you, and then say them out loud. Say them out loud so many times that it becomes second nature, almost like saying them is equivalent to your taking a breath. Take control of the words until you are sure your abuser cannot take them from you and manipulate them.

It is important to do this BEFORE confronting your abuser. It will give you the necessary courage and certainty needed to ensure that you do not waiver in the conversation. Remember, when you are confronting your abuser, the goal is not to argue or yell at them. You want to approach them quietly. This way they know you are serious, and the less hysterical you are in the conversation, the less chance they have to manipulate and turn the situation around.

When you confront your abuser and you are able to speak to them calmly, give them a chance to realize what you are saying. They might need time to process that their own behaviors are abusive. Remember, many abusers do not know what they are doing is emotionally abusive.

If, during your conversation, they still do not back down or admit to their behaviors, use phrases that highlight their behavior as abusive. Stand your ground. This part of the conversation is where an emotional shield might also be helpful.

Some key phrases you might use with someone who is being emotionally abusive are:

- Your stare is not going to intimidate me.
- It is not okay for you to belittle me/call me by that name.
- That story does not embarrass me.
- I will not be coerced into doing something I do not want to do.

The goal of the conversation with your abuser is to come to a resolution, not to start an argument, so be firm but gentle when you are talking to them. Even if you decide to end the relationship, remain steadfast in your reasons why, and do not incite an argument where they can manipulate you.

If you have confronted your abuser and have decided to stay together but you notice that the abusive behavior is continuing, it is time to stress your boundaries. Talk to them again and be very clear about what your boundaries are and where they lie.

Stressing the seriousness of your talk with the abuser can be to instill consequences for breaking boundaries. Let them know that you will not tolerate the behavior anymore. For emotionally abusive situations, an example can be when an abuser forces you to try and do something by making you feel guilty. Be clear with them that you will not do things out of guilt, and they cannot coerce you. Also let them know that the consequence to their actions is that you will not conform to what they want out of fear.

Being clear about your boundaries is one of the best things you can do when you are in an emotionally abusive situation you are trying to fix, but sometimes your words can seem empty.

The hardest part about confronting your abuser can be to stand by your decisions and boundaries. Once you have laid a boundary down for your abuser, it is crucial that you stand firmly by your decision. Let them know what the consequences are and then carry out the consequences if they continue the abusive behavior.

Do not let yourself fall back into the cycle of abuse. This is where having someone to affirm that you are the victim can be helpful. Let a third party who is aware of your situation know what your boundaries are. When they hold you accountable, you are more likely to feel stronger in your decisions, and it will be easier to stand by your decisions with support, even if one of those decisions is walking away from your abuser.

Chapter summary

A lot of information regarding standing up to and talking to your abuser was covered in this chapter. It is never an easy task to sit down face-to-face with someone who has messed with your head— whether they are doing it unwittingly or not. The repercussions of being the victim of emotional abuse can be long-lasting. Let's go over a few key elements about talking to an abuser:

- Wanting to work things out with your abuser is okay.
- An abuser can be an intimate partner, parent, sibling, friend, or even an employer.
- Sometimes you need an emotional shield with you when you are talking to an abuser.

- If you do not want another person present, you can conduct the conversation through the phone.
- Choosing where and when the meeting takes place is crucial to regaining some control that has been taken from you. It is also important to demonstrate to your abuser that you are not going to be manipulated anymore.
- Practice saying how they are abusing you out loud.
- Do not go into the conversation expecting a fight. Try and be calm about the situation. Be gentle but firm when speaking to them.
- Let them know that there are consequences to their abusive behaviors.
- Stand by your consequences and decisions.
- Having someone hold you accountable as the victim can ensure you do not fall back into an emotionally abusive cycle.

Sometimes you can work things out with your

abuser. Therapy can make a big difference in both yours and the abuser's lives. Many relationships in which emotional abuse played a role can be salvaged and worked on. It is not uncommon, and you are definitely not in the wrong if you want to work things out.

But there is a line where people cross into the territory of being too emotionally abusive. In these situations, you will want to find your way out. Maybe you have tried to make it work, or maybe you are just done once and for all, and you want to walk away from the situation. That is okay too. In the next chapter, we will go over how you can safely leave the situation you are in.

Chapter Seven: A Way Out

This is the moment. You have decided that the relationship is over and that it is time to leave. Either your partner had crossed too many lines into abusive territory, or they did not respect your boundaries when you confronted them about their abusive behaviors.

You might remember when I mentioned the fact that when a victim is leaving their abuser, that is the most dangerous time for them. This fact remains true; however, do not be scared. This is why you picked this book up, for support and guidance. That is exactly what I am about to give you.

Firstly, know that what you are doing is not an easy decision. It takes time, pain, and loss to get to the stage that you are. Removing yourself from your emotional abuser's web can be tricky and difficult. If children are involved, it can make the situation more complicated, but it can still be done.

Secondly, know that your safety, emotionally and physically, should be your priority. My goal for this chapter is to give you a guideway to getting yourself safely out of an abusive situation. I know it can be concerning, but you have made it this far.

You have been on quite the journey. You learned about some common misconceptions when it comes to emotional abuse. You have also learned what signs to look out for in your relationships if you are being emotionally abused. If you are the friend of someone you are concerned about, then you have learned that the best thing you can do is be there for them. Do not cut them out of your life because they cannot leave their situation on your schedule.

Maybe you learned that you are the abuser. Hopefully, once you learned that information, you took advantage of my suggestions and spoke to a therapist regarding your issues. You also need to be upfront and honest with your partner about what you have been doing. Remember, it does not have to be the end of the relationship, but you do have to put in the work to learn how to modify your abusive behavior.

Leaving with Children

For those that have children with their abuser, it is especially complicated and emotional. It can be a tough choice to decide to remove your children with you. Keep in mind, though, that children are not immune to emotional abuse. If the abuser is not abusing them, too, they can still see and feel the effects emotional abuse has on you.

Some emotional abusers threaten to take your kids away from you if you leave. If you are in a relationship with an abuser who has crossed many boundaries, then you might have already heard their threats. There are lots of tactics that abusers use in order to put your children in between the two of you. These tactics may include trying to turn the children against you, emotionally abusing the children, taking the children and not returning them to you, and even calling immigration—depending on your status—to have the state remove your children from your care.

I know you might be freaking out, but you need to know what to expect and look for when planning to leave your abuser. Relax. Breathe. You need to devise a safety plan.

Safety planning is crucial when you are trying to leave an abuser. A safety plan is a plan of action you come up with, sometimes with help, that can help you map out how to handle dangerous circumstances and react to abusive situations.

Remind your children that their job is to stay safe and not to protect you. Have a place where they can safely meet up and a code word that lets them know when it is safe to leave their meet-up place. Direct your children where and how to get help if it is not safe.

Pack a bag with emergency items for you and your children. Include all their important documents. If you do not have a safe place to store it, leave the bag with a friend or someone you trust. Remember that there are family advocates and shelters that can help you and give you advice. If you do not know about the resources in your town, go to the National Domestic Violence website, and you can chat with someone who will help you out.

Memorize numbers and have your children do it too if they can, just in case you are left without a phone. Understand that if you do leave with your abuser's children, custody is an issue. It is vital you speak to a lawyer, and you know your options. You do not want to break any laws or have to keep running once you get away from your abuser.

Creating a Safety Plan

For anyone in an abusive situation, it is important to create a safety plan. It can be one you write down or even one that you memorize and keep in your head. There are a few vital steps I will walk you through to help you with your safety plan.

If you are being emotionally abused, keep any evidence you can, as emails and messages are your best friends in this situation. If they threaten you, save the messages. Take pictures of them if you have to.

Tell someone what is happening to you. It does not have to be a friend or family member. Reach out to someone who professionally deals with abusive situations if you have to. Telling someone ensures that you are not the only person that knows about your situation.

If you can, try setting money aside. With an abuser that controls your finances, this can be hard. Ask your family or friends, if you can, to keep money aside for you.

When leaving, make sure that you have some important information such as your identification on you. It is a good idea to have legal documents with you too, such as your marriage license or deed to a home if you share a home with your abuser. These can also include medical records or work permits.

Know your emergency numbers. Family and friends are good to know, but memorize your local police department's number and other emergency services as well. They can come in handy.

Once you leave an abusive situation, change your routine. Switch work schedules and change your phone number. Do not stay in the same routine your abuser was accustomed to. Consider renting a post office box for your mail so that your abuser cannot track you down that way. If you have a restraining order, keep a copy of it on you.

It is vital that once you remove yourself from the

situation, you surround yourself with people who are emotionally supportive. Set achievable goals for yourself and then work towards them. Focus on your recovery.

Treat yourself kindly. When you are coming from an emotionally abusive situation, it can be easy to forget that you need to be kind and gentle with yourself as well. Give yourself time to heal and remember that you are worth saving.

If you are a friend or loved one, your best safety plan is to be supportive. Listen to them and help connect them to resources. Do not share their location or other private information with anyone else or on social media. Helping a victim you love can be frustrating when they do not do what you think they should. Be patient; everyone processes abuse in his or her own ways.

Chapter summary

This chapter was mainly about finding a way out for yourself. Some of the most important tips to remember are to:

- Make a safety plan.

- A safety plan can be for you and/or your children.
- Try your best not to leave important documents behind.
- Change your routine. Change places you shop and visit.
- Lean on friends and family.
- Give yourself time to heal.
- Be kind to yourself.

I will say it one more time, because to someone who has been emotionally abused, this is the most important information you will hear: be kind to yourself. As you chart your way forward, you need to nurture some social skills to help you along the way as you meet new people. We shall have a look at how to develop some social skills in the chapters that follow.

Chapter Eight: Nurture Your Relationships

Relationships we develop, both professionally and personally, define us. Whether it's with a parent, sibling, spouse, child, boss, team, coworker, or business partner, you should never be complacent. You should put in time to show people that you care about them.

Making important relationships a daily priority eases your work and increases your productivity. Trust and mutual respect are the products of well-preserved relationships.

Preserving relationships requires hard work and continuous effort like everything good in life, but they are worth it. In order to keep healthy relationships, several laws must be followed. They include the following:

1. *Communication.* Perhaps the most important factor for any relationship to strive is healthy communication. Most people find it unnatural to talk about relevant things in their lives with other

people. However, people can't read minds. Even those that care about us wouldn't relate and understand us if they couldn't tell what was going on in our lives. For healthy relationships to strive, communication is an important pillar.

2. *Vulnerability.* People avoid communication in order not to look vulnerable. Don't be afraid to share your thoughts, emotions, fears, and worries in life, however uncomfortable it might feel. Openness in a relationship paves the way for more love, closeness, and a stronger connection. Fight every urge of holding things from people you relate to.

3. *Self-awareness.* Self-awareness is the state of knowing one's own character and feelings. It involves observation of your own actions and keeping track of your own thoughts. With self-awareness, you realize that the source of your feelings, thoughts, words, and actions are from past experiences. You are able to communicate better, and vulnerability doesn't scare you. Meditation and therapy can improve your self-awareness.

4. *Emotional intimacy*. Emotions have a way of haunting you if they are not dealt with. You can't keep a healthy relationship if you can't handle your emotions. Being able to access your emotions and express them in a healthy manner strengthens your relationships. Being comfortable with your emotions makes you more sincere and helps you in returning to a healthy state of mind.

5. *Integrity*. Integrity is the quality of being honest and having strong moral principles. No matter the situation, you should keep your integrity both for yourself and your partner in the relationship. You should align your actions with your values. Always keep your word—your word is your bond. When you find yourself acting in the interest of others, ask yourself if you're still the person you would like to be. Jerk yourself back into reality. Lacking integrity in a relationship causes unnecessary hurt to other people. Showing a lack of integrity is always the easy way out. Be strong in your virtues and more people be attracted to your point of view.

6. *Taking responsibility*. Blaming others for

the trouble you're in prevents you from moving forward. Playing the victim makes yourself and loved ones expect others to handle your own shortcomings. It takes power from you, as there is always something you can do about your situation. If you're in a sticky situation, there's a high probability that you had a hand in getting yourself in it. When conflicts arise in relationships, two people are always to blame. Both of you are responsible for making it better. Blaming each other will find you in the same situation time and again since you get complacent waiting for the other person to change for the both of you.

7. *Balance between space, freedom, and connection.* To make a great partner in a relationship, you may require time alone occasionally. This allows you to reconnect stronger when you find yourself. When seeking some alone time and space, always remember to keep others in the loop to remind them that you still care. Some alone time allows you to meditate and gain a new perspective on your issues. Only then can you share your perspective with

the people you care about.

8. *Taking a stand.* Many people can't stand up for themselves in the face of adversity. This might be due to childhood trauma from an overaggressive guardian or bullying at a young age. Always remember that you have boundaries and a sense of self-preservation. It's easy to lose yourself in your partner in a relationship that is dangerous. The other person may breach your boundaries, and not standing up for yourself may cause you to resent them. If you don't respect yourself, other people will lose respect for you, which builds an unhealthy relationship. You should be courageous enough to demand respect for your boundaries, even if it means getting a little angry. Never take abuse lying down.

9. *Resilience.* This is the ability to recover quickly from shock or a crisis. With the ups and downs of any relationship, life requires you to have a little stamina and resilience to keep it going. Running at the first sign of trouble is a dangerous mentality. Adopt a boxer's fighting mentality. You are in it till the twelfth round—don't give up on the title. Conflict

in relationships is normal, but endurance is required.

10. *Having a mentor*. Mentors are meant to motivate us through hard times. When you're in a pickle that you can't seem to get out of, there are always experts who have written books about it or workshops on the same topic. Read the books and interact personally with them, if you can. There is always knowledge to be gained. Mean to apply the gained information and don't just going through the motions for the sake of reading or listening to it.

Qualities of a Nurturing Person

1. *Self-control*. A person who exhibits control over certain behaviors plays a great role in a healthy relationship. Paying attention in the moment and practicing patience over desires builds self-control. If a person is always asking you to repeat what you just said because they can't help but check on their Facebook account, they don't value your relationship.

2. *High self-esteem.* When a person has high self-esteem, they aren't looking to the people in their life for constant gratification. Having a healthy relationship with yourself leaves you with enough energy and time to work on relationships with others.

3. *Openness to personal growth.* Any relationship is a chance for both parties to grow as individuals. Space for growth is in handling conflicts as well as learning to balance someone else's needs with your own. Relationships aren't always smooth sailing. For the survival of a healthy relationship, one must be willing to learn and change on mistakes.

4. *Sense of humor.* A sense of humor is the ability to remain happy even in distress, usually by finding fun in your tough situation. When you appreciate when to make your partner smile, you qualify as having a sense of humor. You don't have to be a comedian. A good partner identifies when to make the other person laugh to release some stress and anxiety. However, humor shouldn't be used to avoid a difficult situation requiring serious

conversations.

5. *Maturity.* Most people mistake a grown-up act for maturity. Maturity of the mind entails being careful with your intentions and thorough in your thoughts. Learning from past mistakes in relationships is real maturity. A mature person is ready to find solutions to past challenges that may interfere with present relationships.

6. *Honesty.* Honesty excludes blowing out someone else's candle or commenting on their poor choice of clothing, even though it might be true. Honesty in a relationship is about important matters and openness on wants and needs. Being vulnerable enough to share your expectations in relationships shows honesty.

7. *A positive attitude.* An optimistic view builds a healthy and happy relationship. A good attitude toward your relationships motivates you to work on them to be better. Happiness, like any other emotion, rubs off to the other parties in a relationship. A negative attitude may leave the other party feeling disappointed and depressed.

8. *Gratitude.* This is the desire or feeling to express one's thanks. A thank-you note can be enough to reinforce the other party's investment in the relationship. It might be a small act, but it's the thought that counts. The person feels appreciated and valued as a stakeholder in the "partnership." With gratitude, you develop ways to be nice to the other person; hence, the relationship develops stronger bonds and happiness.

Relationships require hard work to be preserved. Communication and vulnerability between involved parties are crucial as they create openness. It is this openness that creates a stronger bond between partners. You should know your character and feelings, and you should be able to express your feelings in a healthy way. It is in expressing these emotions that both partners understand each other better. We should always stand our ground while maintaining integrity in the relationship that builds trust and respect. Remember, we are all human, and we make mistakes. Always take responsibility for your actions, and work through the relationship, even through tough times. Although the best way to improve any relationship is together, consider taking some time alone to work through your issues. It will give you a new perspective before you reconnect. If all doesn't work, consider talking to a professional or taking advice from a person you respect along those lines.

In order for a relationship to work, you need to work on yourself first. It's tempting to betray the people who trust us, but we should exercise self-control and honesty. High self-esteem is an attractive virtue. Don't depend on other people to make you feel good about yourself; they will always come short. For a happy relationship, you should look at life with a positive eye and always keep a sense of humor as stress can derail any relationship. Maturity is required in decision-making while being ready and willing to learn in order improve on yourself. Lastly, always remember to say thank you.

Sometimes you may feel out of place, like you don't belong, especially with the people around you. Almost everyone has been overwhelmed by these feelings at some point in their lives. We shouldn't let these feelings get us down as they aren't unique to us.

At best, it's just a phase where relating to

anybody else feels like a bother, especially if you are going through some things. At times, you may have to see a psychiatrist, as it may be much worse. Sometimes doing your own thing is cool. Remember, nobody ever reached their goal trying to impress other people. However, even when being independent, you may worry you're not fitting in.

In this era of digital social media, everyone is always on his or her phone. Even with everybody's terrible lack social lives, you can't help but feel left out when nobody checks out your timeline or likes your status updates on Facebook.

When you feel like an outcast at school or can't seem to fit in at the office, the digital world is the last nail on the coffin. You may start to wonder if your "independent life" is due to circumstance and not a choice.

Being a lone wolf isn't imprinted in our DNA. Humans are historically predisposed to feel the need to belong. The feeling of not being able to reside may, therefore, affect both our functionalities and states of mind. To remedy this and feel like part of the society again, you may need to understand what the root cause is.

Being an Outsider

Sensitivity as a young child. Outsiders may exhibit social awareness as early as childhood, realizing people's reactions to their words and actions. One in five children is socially shy. Being on guard makes them exhibit almost no interactions with strangers, and they tend to cry more. Half the number break their social reticence by childhood, but the rest may seclude themselves even into early adulthood.

Family stress as a child. Growing up in a dysfunctional family may cause the child to be alienated. This is mostly due to role confusion, which primarily affects younger siblings. Dysfunctionality may be due to divorce, parental favoritism, or family estrangement.

Being misunderstood. Younger siblings are more prone to feeling misunderstood. Growing up in confusion, they often go unnoticed, hence the feeling of being misunderstood. As the situation worsens in school, you may notice behavioral changes, which may result in further alienation.

Resenting authority. Outsiders are often rebels. Their instinct makes them go against any form of authority. This may be the parents, teachers, or anyone in uniform. Outsiders may be reluctant to acknowledge their power, questioning the why to the what, which may grow even into adulthood. Sometimes it is just a rebellion without a cause.

Distorted empathy. Outsiders are cynical and often exhibit distrust and disrespect about social norms. This may explain why they root for the bad guys in a society, which includes criminals and terrorists. Even though they may never go such lengths, they can relate to the feeling of isolation, anger, and frustration that can lead to criminal deeds.

Identity problems during adolescence. Adolescence is filled with challenges and embarrassing moments that may lead to isolation from our peers. This causes an identity crisis well into adulthood. Early or late puberty around their peers may cause separation and deviant behavior in many adolescents. The most affected are girls whose adolescence is setting on early and boys whose puberty is delayed.

Remedies to Feelings of Being an Outsider

Here are tips to get over not belonging:

1. Stop being hard on yourself. Nothing is wrong with you when it's hard to fit in. Nobody can make you feel inferior without your consent. Let go of your emotional inhibitions, and you will fit in just fine. Beating yourself up is never part of the solution; it only digs you deeper in the hole. It's not a crime to feel like you don't belong; you can do your own thing. While trying to conform to everyone else's standards, you lose sight of your ambition and goals. Unique people always have something special to offer. Don't be afraid to make an impact as who you are. We are all destined for greatness, only not as other people.

Never settle for being like everyone else. Changing who you are to fit in is a wrong move. Gaining other people's approval isn't worth losing who you are. Strive to be your absolute best. Thinking you can never be good enough, no one likes you, and you will never fit in doesn't help. All it does is get you stuck on negativity, and you may never move forward. It is only on repetition that these thoughts manifest to you. Instead, meditate on your desires, what you enjoy doing, and focus on exploring them further. Soon you will let go of the negativity, and you can focus on the positive you can undertake. Only then will you gain the power to turn your life around.

2. Be comfortable with yourself. Think about your role model, why they are inspirational. Notably, you admire them because they are like no other and never try desperately to fit in. They share their unique character with pride with the rest of society. It's actually a good thing to be different.

You are unique in your personality and capabilities. Your amazing gifts, thoughts, and ideas only manifest when you chase after self-happiness and doing what you like. Be comfortable in your skin with everything that makes you unique. Avoid self-sabotaging by staying angry from past events and limiting yourself by thinking you aren't good enough. Do some soul searching about the source of your unhappiness. Explore those negative feelings and get rid of self-limiting beliefs. Set goals to be happy, stay healthy, and be confident. With inner peace, you are stronger and much wiser.

The more you are comfortable with yourself, so are other people. With self-respect, you gain respect from others. When you focus on yourself, you move far beyond the peers you felt the need to fit in with. You realize that it's a mistake to always try to fit in. By gaining comfort in your skin, you become more accepting of others and open to new ideas. When you're terrified of being different, you never come up with new ideas, and you are passed on by exciting opportunities.

Enjoy every moment as you understand yourself and focus on finding people with the same attitude for life. When worrying about the opinions of a few, you miss out on the beauty of the world. Focus on your experiences and chasing after your goals.

3. Let go of past anger. Our past hurt may cause us to repel people as you feel you can't relate to anyone. In our anger, we can only expect the worst from others. Once you let go of past anger, it becomes easier to get along with others as you are more comfortable with yourself. You stop focusing on what they think about you. People are repelled from you if you give off an aura of anger. In the end, you may get along with angry people like yourself. Instead of losing your temper, focus on the greater good. Staying angry takes up much of your energy and time, which you could redirect into achieving your dreams and bettering yourself.

4. Focus on what you want and what you desire. Finding fulfillment in life diverts your attention from the negativity of not fitting in. You can do this by setting goals, learning new things, and chasing after your dream. Travel to new destinations and engage in new activities to prevent you from being caught up in the negativity. Find happiness from the pool of inspiring and incredible things the world has to offer. Forcing yourself to fit in can only bring you temporary joy. Stay true to yourself. Finding your passion gives you a sense of self-worth. In respect, you gain recognition from everyone around you. With self-motivation, you reach greater heights than you ever imagined.

5. Remember that you are not alone. We have all felt like we don't belong at some point in life; you are not the only one. Ironically, even the most socially capable in our view have felt lacking when encountering the need to belong. Whenever you feel like you don't fit in at social gatherings, look around. Someone else may be in the same predicament as you are. Go over and say hi. You might as well make friends as you get over that feeling. Even the most exceptional people that ever lived felt out of place.

Our evolutionary history explains the need for us as humans to belong. However, fitting in shouldn't preoccupy you into reducing your self-worth when it proves hard. We should identify the reasons behind feelings of being an outsider. Past experiences scarring our social lives should be recognized. It is always easy to let go.

Focusing on trying to fit in diverts our attention from our goals and dreams. Chase after your dreams, and increase your self-worth. We are all unique with different identities. Acceptance from others is built on self-acceptance. In reaching your goals, self-motivation is incomparable. You can only be your best if you accept your differences and shine on your strengths. Always remember, changing yourself to fit in is not worth it. If they can't take you for you, they aren't worth your attention.

A lot of people claim they get so angry that they can't control it. When asked if they punched the person who made them angry, in most cases the response is negative. Considering such instances shows that, however angry you may get, it's never out of control.

Don't beat yourself up for getting angry, but never let yourself fly off the handle. Anger should be expressed consciously for both your mental health and physical well-being. Hiding your anger deep inside of you could make you sick if it is not expressed.

Unfortunately, our society today promotes avoiding our emotions, including anger. Anger expression is never taught. Our fear of expression could also emanate from past experiences of unhealthy expressions of anger. However, stuffing up your anger is worse.

The notion that we should avoid our negative emotions is absurd. Scream into a pillow to feel better. Pretending that some things don't get to us isn't healthy. Acceptance goes a long way in solving issues. Don't fight against your own feelings. Soon you will discover that there are healthy ways to deal with it; it doesn't have to be that bad.

Role of Anger

Getting angry usually relays an important message meant for good, but others may feel offended. Often, we get angry in an effort to be heard only to destroy relationships in the process.

In intelligent communication, any form of aggression corrodes your true intent.

Communicating with passive aggression is worse, as opposed to popular belief. Passive aggression may seem innocent from your words, but they are vicious. Most people opt for passive aggression, but it breaks connections. Therefore, you should consider a better strategy for better understanding people. Lately, people are taking to Twitter more and more often for those indirect jabs.

Immediate Anger Expression is Exceptional

Often, we find ourselves mad but can't remember how those feelings started. That is why it is advisable to express your feelings as they come; it helps the negativity go away faster. Extinguish the fire immediately when you see smoke; waiting for the inferno doesn't do you any good. The same can be said for your feelings—handle them as they emerge.

Reasons for You to Express Emotions Immediately

- *They become more intense when you wait.* Contemplating your emotions magnifies their intensity. Getting rid of these emotions immediately saves you from more stress. It's easier to handle things before they blow up. People give advice on waiting when you're angry so that you don't regret later. You regret actions and not feelings. Never be afraid to express what you feel.

- *There are better ways to understand.* Sharing your feelings immediately removes ambiguity over what made you mad or who did what. It just happened. Bottling up your emotions can occasionally set you off by minor issues. Confusion over the source of the sudden emotions only creates new conflict.

- *It's an opportunity for clarification in case of a misunderstanding.* Most times, being angry with someone emanates from a misunderstanding. You may have interpreted them the wrong way. A simple explanation about the issue clears the air.

- *It's unlikely to be fixed unless something is said.* The receiving party and everyone else around you aren't mind readers. They could never know how you feel unless you tell them. They may be part of the solution; there is no point in holding back.

- *You don't have to fake it.* It's draining to hide your emotions with your actions. Being true to yourself is important for both your emotional health and a healthy state of mind.

- *You don't have to bottle your emotions.* Avoiding your emotions doesn't make them disappear. On the contrary, stuffed-up emotions have been linked to several physiological ailments. They include depression, asthma, anxiety, high blood pressure, and infections.

- *You are more comfortable with your feelings.* When you are aware of your emotions and are able to express them, you become comfortable enough to obtain information crucial in decision making.

- *Your feelings change.* The best way to get rid of negative emotions is to get over them. You only get over them by recognizing and expressing them in a healthy way. Psychologists agree that talking your heart out completely, although you may be angry, manifests positive feelings. You always feel better if you talk to a friend.

- *You create stronger bonds.* People avoid their emotions in fear of being rejected. Ironically, being honest and vulnerable provide a strong base for good relationships. You know the other person better with their expression of themselves. You also get to know how your actions affect the other person.

- *Your family and friends start doing the same.* People close to you follow your lead if you express your feelings freely. With the same benefits, they become emotionally healthier. This makes you closer to them.

Expressing Your Anger While Conserving Relationships

In the event you are angry, neither passive aggression nor the extreme direct approach is advised. They destroy your relationships. Instead, follow the guides below:

- *Become self-aware.* Never be too quick in expressing your frustration. Instead, take a minute for cooler heads to prevail. When our emotions are running high, we are never thinking straight. Be conscious of what's really going on for more effective communication. Take a walk, exercise, meditate, or pray to regain your composure for a better perspective on the whole situation.

- *Understand your emotions.* Often we confuse hurt and sadness with anger, which might be easier to express. Frustration could well be pain, sorrow, or rejection. Pinpoint the real emotion you feel in order to communicate with honesty, hence, more effectively.

- *Be on the lookout for misplaced blame.* Always find the root of your anger. You may just be hungry, going through stuff, exhausted, or lacking sleep. Don't dish it out to the next innocent person that crosses your path. Sometimes it's easier to assign blame, as we find it taxing than to think of the real reason behind our frustrations. However, it only drives people we care about away. Nothing is resolved until the real burning issue is tackled.

- *Be curious.* Curiosity helps us see the bigger picture. In our frustrations, we forget there is the other person's perspective, and you lose this by only thinking of yourself. Try moving away from being self-centered and ask why the other person made you mad. It couldn't have been intentional. Confronting them doesn't provide real reasons. Care a little, as they might be going through something you can help them with. Try understanding that the other person doesn't aim to hurt you on purpose. You may even get over your anger easily with a little understanding.

- *Be compassionate.* Don't be quick to assume the worst of people. Try to understand what they're going through, along with their point of view. Always show respect for people's feelings and understand why they act in a certain way. This opens up the opportunity for effective communication. With compassion and empathy, your relationships get deeper. Aggressive communication makes people angry and defensive in return. Giving people an opportunity to share their perspective makes them respect yours even more.

- *Communicate with skill.* In an effective communication, skills like compassion, curiosity, and compromise go a long way. Don't just stop at sharing your feelings, or you'll be self-centered. Go a step further and ask the other party to share with you. Show interest and be ready to compromise. Never accuse someone without their side of the story.

How to Deal with Passive-Aggressive People

- *Call them out.* Never give anyone a pass for showing aggression in any way. You might as well ask what they meant with their words. People don't expect to be called out when they are passive-aggressive. Ask more question to get to the root of what bothers them. A grown-up conversation over how they feel would be one way to show them another way.

- *Ignore them.* Even though the other party is trying to get a point across, you shouldn't be drawn into their hostile attitude. As soon as you engage, you enter the same state of mind, which is unhealthy. You live happier by letting such situations go.

- *Show forgiveness and a little compassion.* Tension and frustration cause one to show aggression, either directly or passively. Don't be so hard on such a person; they are already hurt. Just set boundaries for your own sake, but forgive them and wish them good vibes.

- *Invite them to share their own feelings and perspectives.* Show the other party that there is a better way of handling their aggression. Leading by example works best. When you express your negative emotions, ask them to do the same. Soon they move away from passive-aggressive tactics that only worsen their situations.

In conclusion, it's okay to be mad and frustrated. The important matter is to express it in a healthy way. A proper expression of your negative emotions can leave you feeling better. Funny enough it might as well be a misunderstanding needing clarification. It's not healthy to be playing okay but you're not. Bottled emotions can make you sick emotionally and physically too. You see the benefits as soon as you learn to communicate emotions effectively.

While it is important to express your feelings as they emerge, bear in mind you have relationships to conserve. It's not worth it to lose friends because you got mad. Apply communication skills. Don't be self-centered. Inquire and be ready to listen and understand the other person's perspective. As you realize communicating truly has advantages, your family and friends will follow suit and reap the same benefits. Therefore, it is important to notice people with aggressive communication and show them a better way, or just avoid interacting with them altogether.

Chapter Nine: Be Empathetic

How you interact with your family, friends, colleagues, and romantic partners largely depends on your social skills. However, if you want to build good social skills, empathy is one of the best to incorporate.

Empathy is defined as "the ability to acknowledge and share the feelings and experience of another person." In the way of explanation, it is expressed as putting yourself in someone else shoes, feeling and understanding what they go through, and seeing yourself and the rest of the world from their point of view. You can't understand why someone did whatever he or she did or acts a certain way until you imagine yourself in his or her position, walking in his or her skin, and considering things from his or her perspective.

Empathy is not present to everyone; some people can watch through the latest news on terrorism attacks at night and just roll over and fall asleep.

Whereas a large percentage of people can't watch the same story at night since the news brings pain and suffering deep to their hearts and, at the end, distracts their minds from falling asleep. Empathy is expressed as "the psychological identification with or vicarious experiencing of feelings, thoughts, or attitudes of another person." Remember that you need to understand the difference between empathy and sympathy. Sympathy is a feeling used to communicate consolation, pity, or sorrow for someone else who is going through misfortune. Sympathy doesn't require your understanding of someone's sorrows or how they are journeying through their lives.

Who is an Empath and how is It Different from Being Empathetic?

An empath can be identified as a person who is emotional, sensitive, and always trying to feel the struggles of the world. However, the benefits of being an empath are that you are always there to care for another person and offer an extra hand to help out. Empathy can be exhausting since it consumes most of your feelings. An empath can't apply the same filters that others do to control their stimulation. They are characterized by an extremely sensitive, hyper-reactive system; therefore, they take in all the positive and negative energies around them.

The Understanding of Empathy in Society

The basic foundation of *compassion* is emotional self-awareness, which in today's culture, is rarely nurtured. How many times are boys told to be strong and hold their tears? How often have you heard girls being shut down and told to sit down and told they're "acting crazy?" How many times do you hide your feelings by convincing yourself you aren't supposed to feel that way? In our current culture, a normal person usually cares less and doesn't give much empathy toward others because he or she prioritizes on everything else, rather than their emotional well-being. Nevertheless, there isn't a healthy balance between the negation of people's feelings and acknowledgment of feelings. To cope, you need to disassociate both of them.

Learning Empathy

Just like driving a car or riding a bicycle, empathy

skills can be taught; others even learn it very early in life. It means developing a mental awareness to achieve someone else's perspective. If you are patient and you want to relate with one another, often clinics offer empathy training programs. You can start the learning process by simply asking others how they feel and pay attention to the replies.

Consequently, empathy can be an awkward feeling to express. In the case where you don't understand how it feels to be in someone else's shoes and you don't care, you can't close your eyes and get it. You will be blocking your emotional feelings; therefore, you can't feel for others when your emotions are shut down.

Naturally Learning Empathy

People with antisocial personalities, autism, or schizophrenia are faced with empathy impairments. However, some undiagnosed children and adults are suffering from low empathy levels. Some categories of people are genetically qualified to be highly empathetic while others aren't. You develop empathy from childhood by observing how other people express it.

You may be the one receiving the empathy occasionally and appreciate it for the comfort it brought. Similarly, you can express empathy to another person and enjoy positive responses, such as a hug, acknowledgment, or even praise, which builds your social skills.

In children, the more empathy you share to them and they observe on others, the more they build relationships with other children. If you are a parent and want to teach your children empathy, you can start by explaining your emotions during a festive event, such as Thanksgiving. You can engage them in a conversation to discuss their own feelings as well as others. Teach them how to recognize the link between events and emotions. For example, "When I heard my puppy was going to die, at first I felt startled, then speechless, and eventually sadness overwhelmed me."

As a parent, you can lead by example by showing your empathy when the child is experiencing strong emotions such as anxiety, worry, fear, surprise, and so on. For instance, you can ask your child questions to express their inner feelings, such as, "How do you think your classmate felt when you tore his books?" Don't forget to applaud the child for expressing empathy to another person.

Self-Taught

In this life, there are more opportunities for you to enhance your empathy. You can improve your empathy level by teaching yourself. In fact, you can start by observing how other people express their emotions. You can read signs such as facial expressions, voice intonation, postures, conversation content, and current position.

If you put yourself in someone else's situation, you take an extra step to enhance your empathy. If you get to know and understand a person's emotions and gently express it to another person, you are lucky to get a positive result, which is the first step to enhance your empathy level fully.

Increasing empathy is beneficial to most individuals. However, there are groups of people who gain nothing from increasing their empathy. For combat soldiers and police officers, their work environment requires them to be emotionally stable and strong to perform professionally. Meaning, improving their empathy doesn't have any benefits to them on duty.

Learning Empathy as an Adult

Are you looking to expand your empathy level? Then you are in the right place. Empathy is appreciating another for who they are and not just what they do to you. You appreciate that even if you undergo the same misfortune, you may have a different perspective. Additionally, empathy is how you show love to others. With empathy, you can understand those who show you love for who they are, not whom you conceive them to be. Without empathy, you might assume that other people's needs, feelings, and boundaries are the same as yours. In the end, you make assumptions that can put you in a fix.

To most people, empathy almost comes naturally. However, you can learn to be empathetic by trying out the following steps:

- Take, for instance, your love partner, friend, family, or coworker and examine how their moods and attitudes have been for the past days.
- How are they doing in their daily lives?

What makes them happy, sad, angry, or anxious?

- How positively are you contributing to their lives?
- How are you going to enhance this person's position?

Let's look at an example. In your marriage, your partner has been acting strangely and angry lately. He or she arrives home from their daily commute from work exhausted, and they just want to lie down. The previous night, all he or she did was complain about the job being stressful that you barely spoke about other aspects in your marriage, and, if you did talk, he or she was still ruminating about their daily commute.

Now, what if you decide to snap at him or her and argue that you also have a daily commute that is much longer than his or hers, or even get angry when he or she doesn't ask you about your day? At the moment, that might be the truth, and it will make you feel better. On the other hand, it is not a helpful response. It will instead worsen things between you both and even destroy your relationship. A positive response will result in a stable bond. Here is an illustration of the empathy exercise in real practice.

- Consider your partner.
- Think about how stressed out your partner has been for the past week.
- Think what might be the cause of the stress. Has he or she failed to perform within the given deadline? Did his or her acquaintance do anything that agitates him or her? Was the recent promotion given to another person and that's why he or she is so upset? You might not get the correct answers to your questions, but be sure to know that if your partner comes home from work angry, there must be something happening.
- Look into the last couple of days and identify the things you might have said or done to contribute to your partner's situation. You may not be the reason behind it, but what have you done to handle the situation? Are you making it better or worse? Put yourself in their same shoes and imagine having a hard time at work. How will you feel to arrive home only for your partner to snap back at you

for complaining about your job?

- Lastly, consider a solution to improve your partner's position. You may decide to buy a gift or even cook a favorite meal. Choose the solution that will boost your partner's mood, not what you'd like to be done to you in the same scenario.

To know if you are empathetic when talking to someone, consider the following empathy checklist:

- Have complete attention to the other person you are talking to.
- Use necessary gestures and facial expressions, such as eye contact, when talking to show you are listening.
- Show your willingness to listen without sarcasm or rejection. If you find yourself bored or annoyed, ask for a break to ease things out.
- Confirm what they are telling you by asking questions, to show that you understand what they are saying, or repeat what they say in your own words.

- Value their emotions. In case you don't stand on the same ground, appreciate their opinions by respecting their right to have a different idea from what you are wishing.

How strong your relationship is with others contributes to your happiness and success in your entire life. Learn how to act with empathy toward another person so that they can also do the same to you. Using the empathy exercise and checklist above, you are now ready to learn and practice expressing empathy to another to strengthen your social skills.

Chapter Ten: Building Social Skills

In life, you may have encountered a waiter who suggested a better meal on the menu or a salesperson who went out of their way to get you a good deal. You may relate to having a supportive team leader or an executive who doesn't forget your name. The people mentioned above all have one thing in common, and that is that they excel in social awareness.

Social Awareness

Having an outstanding quality of social awareness requires you to have empathy, organizational awareness, and a sense of service. As projected in the last chapter, empathy involves the ability to imagine another person's needs while sharing in their feelings, concerns, and experiences. *Organizational awareness* is defined by understanding the politics in organizational setups and how they affect the people within them. Service usually requires one to be aware and up to the task in meeting the needs of clients and customers.

In social situations, awareness requires you to anticipate people's wants and to have a plan of communication that is aimed at meeting their specific needs.

I wouldn't go as far as to compare it to manipulation. Manipulation is purposefully calculated to control using unfair means. Social awareness is best described as natural. It aims at taking people's situations and needs into consideration as much as possible. Public speakers and great leaders are expected to be socially aware, as it goes a long way in gaining the support of the masses.

Caring

Scientific American reported research findings showing a deterioration in levels of empathy, which is our ability to relate to other people's feelings, as compared to where they were thirty years ago. This can be explained by the increase in social isolation in our societies today.

The new forms of digital media have paved the way for digital communication, social networking, and even video conferencing. This means it's no longer necessary for one-on-one interactions, making social isolation more rampant.

It has become easy to be negative to others while socializing online, as you don't meet these people face-to-face. This has given rise to a new social menace referred to as cyberbullying. On the other hand, if you don't feel like relating to people's experiences, disengaging is as easy as a touch of a button. You just have to log off or unfriend the person, which is always an easy option.

When paying no attention to the needs and experiences of others, there is bound to be corrosion of trust in society.

If you can't relate to others' thoughts and feelings, you are bound to isolate yourself and, therefore, trust less. Loss of empathy has significant effects, as trust is the cornerstone of successful leadership and partnerships, even in business.

Excessive Empathy?

Too much of something is poisonous. Similarly, lacking the control in our ability to imagine other people's needs while sharing in their feelings, concerns, and experiences is dangerous. It ceases to be an essential skill and tips over to being a burden. Empathy comes easily to others, which is appreciated.

It would be best if you didn't get too involved in sharing other people's problems, as it can leave you emotionally exhausted. Getting occupied with other people's emotions often leads us to neglect our emotional well-being.

On a scale that is lacking emotional intelligence, it is, therefore, advisable to keep your empathy for others in check for your own good.

Empathy = Trust

When you identify people's needs and feelings, they find it easy to put their trust in you. As opposed to being insensitive, you become the trusted one when you can easily relate to people's experiences, their individual needs, and values in the group. This applies in various fields, whether in salesmanship, dealing with the masses, or being leaders in an organization.

Social Awareness Tactics to Improve Your Leadership Skills

Self-awareness is the state of knowing one's character and understanding your feelings. It usually involves looking inward. On the other hand, social awareness requires one to look outward to understand and appreciate others. Social awareness consists of recognizing and relating to other people's feelings.

To be socially aware, you should live in the moment. Clearing your mind of unnecessary thoughts enables active listening and keen observation. Practicing these following eight tactics can improve your social awareness, hence shaping you into a better leader.

Knowing How to Listen

Often we become preoccupied with coming up with a response that we forget to pay attention to what is being said. Good listeners approach a situation with an open mind. It is only after listening that you get the facts of the case and can analyze the emotions involved. Attentive listening gives you more insight into your employees and organization. You quickly pick up new information that makes it easy to run things.

Understanding What Was Said by Repeating It

If appropriate, you should repeat what was said in your own words while asking for more information to create a better understanding. This relays a message to the other person that they have been understood and their opinions have been taken into consideration. This kind of active listening creates bonds of understanding and trust between leaders and their employees.

Paying Attention to the Tone of Voice

Different conclusions can be drawn from the way you say something. Voice sound is a straightforward expression of the speaker's mood and feelings. For instance, when an employee replies enthusiastically with "No problem!" it is portrayed differently than an ambivalent mutter of the same.

Noticing the tone and energy from your employees gets you in tune with their feelings, which is crucial in ethical leadership. It gives you an opportunity to choose a fitting response or course of action. In virtual meetings, you don't have access to the other person's visual cues, hence their tone of voice gives you more insight into their feelings.

Being Keen on Body Language Facial Expressions

Noticing nonverbal cues requires you to be present and paying full attention. Being keen on body language and facial expressions goes a long way in understanding what is said, although it asks for a little extra effort.

For example, it wouldn't be a good idea to set up a meeting with your employee if his body language says it's a bad time. He could be saying yes because you are the boss, but his physical reaction may tell you it's not a good time.

In this instance, you should express that you've noticed the hesitation and reschedule the meeting, asking for suggestions of what time wouldn't be disruptive of his work schedule.

Keeping a Finger on the Pulse of the Office

You should be able to identify the employee's feelings, even without asking. Social awareness requires observational skills. Your awareness of your surrounding sets the pace for your approach in different situations.

A right balance of mood and pace should be maintained in the work environment. Having a sense of the situation on the ground can help you keep that balance with your employees. In the event your team is overwhelmed, you could outsource some of the work. Another way would be to give your employees incentive on overtime to reduce the workload. You can also help your team to focus and prioritize if you feel work is not getting done.

Having an idea of the pace in the office can help you give out reasonable timelines on new projects that have to be handled and who is available and well suited for the job. Knowing the mood enables you to make such decisions easily.

Paying Attention to Details

Always keep your eyes open and ears on the ground to stay connected to your employees. Making regular office rounds is essential in interpreting the mood of your workforce. Showing interest in your employees makes you see them as people. They can relate to you as you relate to them, hence increasing their performance.

Avoiding the Drive-By

Don't be tempted to discuss important matters with your employees as you see them when moving across the room. Drive-by meetings often interrupt the workflow of your employees. When you have a relevant topic to be discussed with your employee, check for social cues pointing to whether they are available. You can also ask them whether it's a good time to talk before you dive right in.

Stop Taking Notes

Taking notes is crucial in a college lecture room, but it has adverse effects when done in a professional setting. You miss a lot when you are busy jotting down notes. Put down your pen and keep your eyes off the paper while in a meeting. This ensures you have ongoing interactions with the involved parties. It is also crucial in staying aware of the mood of the room. Employees may be of the opinion that the topic of discussion is irrelevant to them. If you notice this, you may change the conversation to a more relevant one. Being present may help you identify which topics need more discussion to know the underlying issues when you notice the tension in the room when they are mentioned.

It is important not to let your pride get in the way of your empathy, organizational awareness, and your sense of service to others. Good leaders aren't easy to come by. Listen attentively and observe before you delegate.

Polishing your social awareness skills can go a long way in earning you favor in your day-to-day life. It not only makes you more trustworthy, but you also learn to trust others when you can relate to them. Whether in a leadership position or a lower rank, you gain experience in taking up responsibility and getting things done.

Chapter Eleven: Improve Your Listening Skills

What is listening? It is the ability to receive and make sense of information in a communication process. Listening is the key to an effective communication process. Why is this the case? Without listening, one is not able to receive and interpret information accordingly. This can lead to a frustrated sender.

Listening is so paramount that many top employers provide listening skills training to their employees. They are aware that listening alone can lead to a profitable venture. How is this possible? Excellent customer relations and increased productivity with fewer mistakes are solely dependent on one's listening skills. Therefore, listening skills are critical tools that one should learn to master.

Excellent Listening Skills also have Benefits in our Personal Lives

The ability to listen effectively will automatically increase your number of friends and also enlarge your social circle. This will, in turn, go a long way in improving your self-esteem and confidence, improving your productivity at workplaces or school, and improving your health. Furthermore, studies have shown that while speaking can increase your blood pressure, listening, on the other hand, lowers it.

Listening is not the same as Hearing

Many times, these two words are misunderstood. Hearing is just a physical process whereby voices or sounds enter your ears. This process happens automatically, provided that you do not have any hearing problems. Listening, however, requires more than that. It needs focus and concentrated effort, mentally and sometimes physically as well.

With listening, it is more important to hear in detail. In this case, one does not only listen to the story itself but also looks to the verbal and nonverbal cues made. These cues may include the tone and language used, the flow of the story, and maybe the way the other person uses their body. One's ability to listen effectively is thereby determined by how accurately one can perceive these cues.

Listening, unlike hearing, is not a passive process. The listener should be at least involved in the communication process, be it mentally or even physically.

The Purpose of Listening

There is no doubt that listening is a vital life skill. However, many people do not find listening as an essential skill because they do not see their purpose in their lives. So what is the purpose of listening?

Listening serves some possible purposes. The purposes of listening will depend on the situation and the nature of the communication. Here are some objectives of listening:

1. To specifically focus on the messages being communicated while avoiding distractions and preconceptions.

2. To gain a full and accurate understanding of the speaker's point of view and ideas.

3. To critically assess what is being said.

4. To observe the nonverbal signals accompanying what is being said to enhance understanding.

5. To show interest, concern, and concentration.

6. To encourage the speaker to communicate adequately, openly, and honestly.

7. To develop a selfless approach, putting the speaker first.

8. To arrive at a shared and agreed understanding and acceptance of both sides' views.

Many times we listen in order to formulate ways to respond. This, however, should not be the reason for listening. Listening should be aimed at understanding what is being said and how it is being said. In this way, we can understand the speaker.

How Do You Develop Active Listening Skills?

1. *Face the speaker and maintain eye contact.* Listening in itself is an active process that calls for one's undivided attention. Gazing outside, using one's phone, or carrying out some duties while in a conversation can act as a hindrance to listening.

While in a conversation, you should do your conversational partner the courtesy of facing them and maintaining eye contact. This means avoiding any distractions like the phone or even paperwork. At times, the speaker may not keep eye contact with you, like in the case whereby he or she is embarrassed, shy, guilty, or even uncertain about something. In such cases, you should excuse the partner but stay focused on what they are saying.

2. *Be attentive but relaxed.* After maintaining eye contact, the next step is to relax. It might look awkward when your eyes remain fixed at the speaker throughout the whole conversation. At times, one should look away, but stay attentive.

By attentive, we mean that one should mentally screen out distractions and background noises to listen more effectively. One should also try hard not to focus on the speaker's accent or mispronunciations, because these can also act as distractions to active listening.

3. *Keep an open mind.* How do you keep an open mind? When listening, you should always avoid the temptation of judging whatever your conversational partner tells you. Thoughts like, "That was so rude of you" more often than not distract our listening. This is because you will be focused on your train of thoughts rather than what the speaker is saying.

Another important thing is avoiding jumping to conclusions. It would help if you remembered that the speaker is trying to express feelings or ideas that are in their brains. This means that you do not have the slightest idea of what they could be, so the best way of understanding those feelings is just by listening carefully.

4. *Listen to the words and then try to picture what the speaker is saying.* During listening, it is essential to exercise your brain so that it can stay focused. This exercise is in the form of creating a mental picture of what the speaker is saying. If it is an event, try to visualize the happenings of the event as told by the speaker. It will make your brain and senses stay alert.

You should also try to listen to the words of the speaker. When it is your turn to listen, stop trying to figure out what you will say next. You cannot listen and rehearse at the same time. Instead, you should focus your energy on what the speaker is saying and try to comprehend every word.

5. *Don't interrupt and don't impose your "solutions."* Every person, at one point or other in their childhood, was taught that it was bad manners to interrupt someone else while conversing. Sadly, that lesson is quickly fading away. Interrupting someone usually sends a message that you think you are better or even that you don't care about what your conversational partner is talking about. As a listener, you should also avoid suggesting solutions. Always provide advice when asked for it.

6. *Wait for the speaker to pause so you can ask clarifying questions.* It is reasonable not to understand some things while in a conversation. In such cases, asking questions is usually the best thing to do. However, it would be best if you do not ask questions while the speaker is speaking. Wait for the speaker to pause and then say something like "Pardon, I did not understand that concept about..."

7. *Ask questions only to ensure understanding.* Asking questions is a perfect way of ensuring you understand what the speaker is saying. However, many times you may find yourself asking questions that lead to diversion of the topic. For example, your friend may be narrating about an experience they had in a particular country, and then, in the middle of the story, they mention the name of a long-lost friend that you had. It is normal to find yourself asking questions about the friend. These questions, however, will divert your conversation from the experience your friend had to maybe the life of the long-lost friend. Once this happens, it is usually hard to go back and talk about the original story.

8. *Try and feel what the speaker is feeling.* In listening, you have to "put yourself in the other person's shoes." This means that you should place yourself in the other person's situation. For example, if the speaker expresses joy, you should also be jovial. Express the feelings with facial expressions or even body movement. Communicating with them without feeling anything is as good as not communicating at all. It might sound easy, but it is a hard task that requires energy and concentration. This task, however, will go a long way in improving your

listening skills.

9. *Give the speaker regular feedback.* The idea, in this case, is to give the speaker some proof that you are still following. Jumping in with statements like “Wow!” “What an experience!” or “Breathtaking!” can go a long way in showing the speaker that you are attentive.

10. *Pay attention to what isn’t said (nonverbal cues).* Funnily enough, nonverbal cues help us understand the speaker more than the verbal cues. One can learn a lot from a person by just how they deliver the information. It may be through the telephone or even face-to-face. For example, the tone that one uses while on the telephone can tell one a lot about how they feel. On the other hand, when talking face-to-face, many signs are to be looked out for. Body movements or even facial expressions can make you detect enthusiasm or even boredom.

As we conclude the chapter, listening is an essential skill in life. Listening means being selfless enough to give one an opportunity to express their feelings and ideas. This skill requires one’s attention—both mentally and physically; mentally in that one has to follow what the speaker is saying and also make sense of it. On the other hand, it requires one's physical attention. One should avoid any distractions, like background activities, while in a conversation. Remember that listening is the key to a productive discussion. Always yearning to listen more should be the motive.

Chapter Twelve: Good Communication Skills

Face-to-face conversation is when two or more people physically converse with each other. It is a part of oral communication in which both parties participate in the discussion at once. Therefore, all informal conversations that involve two people who see each other eye to eye are regarded as face-to-face conversations. However, chatting over the phone can't be considered a face-to-face conversation, but as an oral communication form.

Face-to-face communication can be defined as the transmission of a message verbally or nonverbally from the sender to the receiver. Oral communication can be face-to-face or over the phone, yet all types of face-to-face conversations are oral. Let's look at the types of face-to-face conversation for deep understanding.

Types of Face-to-Face Conversation

- Meetings
- Conferences
- Workshops and seminars
- Class lectures
- Art performance on stage
- Public lectures
- Interviews

The Situation where Face-to-Face is Applied

Face-to-face conversation is vital in some conditions. Without it, the message can be irrelevant or won't produce intended results. The following are some of the cases where face-to-face communication is critical.

1. Client Interaction

Service industries mostly apply face-to-face communication with them to build a good relationship with their clients. Regular face-to-face meetings are scheduled for essential cases, as well as the use of e-mail between the sessions. Lawyers, accountants, doctors, human resource managers, and financial advisors engage in face-to-face communication daily due to their nature of work.

If you want to build a good relationship with your clients, first identify what communication method they most prefer using. For instance, lawyers may find out that clients who are proficient in computers prefer virtual communication to face-to-face communication. Sometimes your clients are too occupied for face-to-face communication. Although if you need to seal your relationships with your clients, it is recommended to apply person-to-person interaction.

There are times when you are caught in a scenario that does not allow shortcuts, and it is impossible to arrange for a personal visit. However, there are various communication methods that you can select.

2. Employee Communication

A critical conversation (such as an employee discussing the objectives of your firm, planning the budget, important meetings, and training) should be done face-to-face to increase its effectiveness. During the assessment of employees, the evaluation process should be carried out in person to evaluate the emotions, facial expressions, and strengths of employees.

A job interview is another scenario that employs face-to-face conversation. It would be best if you saw the interviewee to minimize the risks of hiring someone you can't work with effectively. In case the job in question is not that big of a deal and the potential interviewee is geographically far, use Skype to conduct the interview.

Consequently, when you want to hire an independent contractor, such as a web developer, first you can look at his or her sample of work through the internet. Much of the information is available online, even their phone number, which you can use to reach them. You can evaluate the available data and decide if the person is worth hiring.

However, daily conversations should be conveyed

through e-mail or calls. Where calls are used, follow up the discussion with a written document for reference purposes.

3. Negotiations

Conversations between you and your potential manufacturers or clients need to be a person-to-person negotiation. How strong you build the foundation of your relationships will determine how good a deal you are going to score. It would help if you established trust between the two of you by arranging a face-to-face conversation. If you are looking for company manufacturers, you should visit them to see their work and premises, so you can avoid being scammed.

After you have built trust, you can now use, let's say, e-mail, which ensures the conversation is documented. However, e-mail documents are beneficial in generating different reports for legal purposes.

In some few cases, you might know the contractor, so there is no need to build trust because a strong relationship already exists between you two. You can use both e-mail and telephone without meeting them in person and still achieve your objectives.

Features of Face-to-Face Communication

Face-to-face conversation is a casual verbal method of communication with unique characteristics. Below you will find the most significant attributes of face-to-face communication.

- *Informal.* Face-to-face conversations involve the sender and the receiver exchanging messages openly and freely without maintaining any formalities.
- *Straight conversation.* The most significant characteristic of face-to-face communication is the fact that it is very straightforward and direct. Parties involved do not need any medium of communication as they converse directly.
- *Costless communication.* Face-to-face conversations do not need any necessary preparations, thus making it free naturally.
- *Mutual correlation.* Face-to-face conversation is dependent on the bilateral

relationship amid the person sending and the one receiving the messages, hence nobody can intervene.

- *No legal basis.* Face-to-face communication is invisible and not a written form of the conversation, thus it is not lawfully accepted.
- *Used widely.* Mostly, conversations are oral and take place in the form of face-to-face communication. Mainly due to its inherently natural nature.
- *Broadcasting rumor.* Face-to-face conversations aid in the spreading of rumors over and over again. This could generate a bad image of an organization.
- *Direct feedback.* Face-to-face conversations have the advantage of producing prompt and quick responses.
- *Effect of facial expression.* In face-to-face communication, the facial expressions of parties involved have considerable impacts on the whole conversation procedure.
- *Effect of word of mouth.* Verbal communication generates an immense

word of mouth effect that aids to broadcast the positive or negative news regarding anything contained in the message.

Benefits of Using Face-to-Face Conversation

With the invention of social media, faster phone calls, and e-mails, many people are running away from a person-to-person conversation. Although it is the easiest way of communication, face-to-face communications bring many other benefits that should be considered.

1. *Use of body language.* According to studies, 90 percent of human communication involves the use of body language. If a person reacts during a conversation, you can tell what he or she feels by just reading the body language. Apart from the expression of feelings and understanding, direct feedback is also displayed through facial expression. The tone used can also interpret the other person's feelings, which is not possible in other methods of communication. You can even express your reactions, thereby smoothing the

conversation understanding.

2. *It shows how much you value each other.* The effort of meeting the other person face-to-face shows how much you appreciate them. This is seen through the use of facial expression, such as maintaining eye contact when they are talking, which implies that you understand their opinions and are willing to listen to them. Make sure they also listen to you by engaging them with questions or remarks. For instance, when you travel to meet a client, you will show how much money and effort you are willing to devote to your relationship; therefore, a face-to-face conversation offers your complete attention.

3. *Builds strong relationships.* Through face-to-face conversation, you can form a new network of connection which you can use for future endeavors. Whether personal or business relationships, a sense of friendship is developed, which, in turn, establishes a bond of trust in your connection. Face-to-face is an excellent form of persuasion, engagement, and leadership. If you are a busy person, you can engage in face-to-face conversation through the use of video conferencing to conduct meetings, which creates a positive environment and strengthens relationships.

4. *Increases effectiveness.* In the commercial world, efficiency is the key to success. For instance, it will be useful to meet with your team to discuss the details of the project in person, ask questions, write down recommendations, and increase creativity by expanding the project all at once rather than explaining the whole project through e-mail.

5. *Secure private conversation.* In the case where sensitive information is the topic, face-to-face communication is the best form of conversing, since it does not keep evidence. Also, in somber situations, a discussion is handled easily by displaying respect to the other person.

6. *Build trust and credibility.* Use of body language and voice tone in face-to-face conversations sends nonverbal information, which can be interpreted to show the foundation of trust. However, if you are talking in person to the other party, clear explanations and replies to questions are guided by integrity. The more you talk face-to-face, the more you match his or her actions with words, therefore enhancing trust and credibility.

Although verbal communication has many benefits, there are also weaknesses that need to be addressed. For instance, finding time to meet people can be tricky, whereas texting and e-mailing are considered faster, particularly if the other person involved in the communication is in a different country. Besides, communicating face-to-face can be difficult for some people. Also, passing a specific message across to separate people can be hard with face-to-face conversations. However, for you to overcome all these drawbacks, you merely need to set up a video conference.

Main Points to Recall

- If you compare face-to-face communication to electronic methods of communication, you will find that face-to-face conversation has more probabilities to inspire team members.
- Face-to-face conversation lets you grasp a clear picture of how good your message has been comprehended. It also helps you to understand if the team member has any queries regarding what they are being

asked to do.

- Verbal communication is specifically appropriate for discussions, as it provides instant feedback from listeners.
- If the work discussed requires collaboration and coordination, then verbal conversation is the most effective method of communication.
- A face-to-face conversation has one big advantage over electronic communication: It generates a bond of trust between people.

Barriers to Communication

Lately, companies are going to long lengths to get communication training for their employees and managers. The practice increases their results. Effective communication between the staff is directly proportional to the company's success. Nonverbal communication can have adverse effects on the entire line of dialogue. However, when the speaker is well rehearsed and researched, gestures are more likely to be in sync with the speech. Giving out wrong information, misjudging of the situation, or mislaying information can have far more reaching effects than a mismatch in gestures. The audience isn't likely to judge nervousness if the facts of the matter are correct. Preparation makes you less likely to be nervous. Communication is not about make-believe but truth while considering the situation and the audience. The most common causes of miscommunication are the following:

Poor Preparation

Proper preparation is very crucial for any presentation. Most of the time, people research for the information about the project but forget *how* and *when* they should relay this information. When preparing for effective communication, keep the following in mind:

- *Information priority.* Essential information that forms the basis of the topic in the discussion shouldn't be pushed to the back. It should be emphasized and communicated first, however unpleasant. Please make use of communication principles, such as *must*, *should*, and *could*, to reinforce how you say it.

- *Timing and order*. Certain pieces of information relayed to the audience are crucial, and their sequence should be kept logical. The audience can't comprehend some of the data if you communicate in no particular order, either for lack of context or basic understanding. Always have a buildup from the first to the last parts of the conversation for effective communication.

- *Use of consumer-friendly language*. The knowledge of the audience should always be in line with the language of communication. You should avoid the use of jargon to avoid being ambiguous and misunderstood.

- *What should stay with the audience*. Use emphasis, repetition, and visual aids when communicating information that you would wish the audience to remember. Proper preparation is the key in effective communication, as there aren't any shortcuts to it. Tricks wouldn't get past an intelligent listener. It would be best if you always strived to relay that which is of most importance in your subject of communication for the best results.

Lacking Proper Knowledge of the Subject and Forgetting the Essential Details

You've got to have the necessary understanding of every topic you are bound to tackle. Communication is way more comfortable with all the facts in hand. Having fundamental knowledge on the subject in discussion helps you to be precise as you can make sense of the outlined points.

For instance, a list of instructions is more likely to be followed if the main idea behind them is understood and internalized. Guidelines laid out as facts can't be followed mainly because the intended target memorizes them only to forget after a while due to their bulkiness.

Likewise, in a management position, it's impossible to delegate assignments or projects to the project manager or process owner if you can't tell the difference between a development process and a plan.

I would recommend that you sometimes stop and trace your steps back to the basics as part of your preparation. This is a precaution as issues are bound to arise from a misunderstanding when things are not adequately explained.

Unforeseen Reactions: Shallow Thinking

Contemplating your words before you say them is crucial. Moreover, it's always wise to consider how they are mentioned and how the other party will interpret them. The speaker's point of view doesn't always paint the whole picture.

Consider a leader saying to an employee, "Tidy up the office. We have auditors coming in today." From the speaker's point of view, it's a problem averted. However, the employee might feel some nagging, as he might be busy with an unfinished project. After all, to them, they keep things in order. Moreover, the statement emphasizes the tidiness for the auditor's sake and not for the order of the day.

Always consider the following in anticipation of the reaction:

- *The current situation.* Consider the

employee's condition. That is, are they currently working on a project and have they been putting in a lot of extra hours? If so, delegating an additional project to them might not be called for. The management's take on the matter should also be considered to avoid stirring still waters.

- *The listener's attitude.* The listener's attitude toward the subject matter could assist you in anticipating their reactions. A positive attitude may as well predict their agreement with you.

- *Potential counterarguments.* Consider how the listener would reply to your statements. It could either be in the reinforcement of your view or an expression of their opinion that doesn't necessarily see eye to eye with yours. In either case, you can work out a proper response. Preparations for effective communication should always cover the anticipation of the reactions to your statements. It can take only five seconds. Consulting a colleague as a third party is advised if you deem it essential.

Other causes of lousy communication include:

Judging Other People

This kind of behavior is as a result of self-righteousness on the speaker's part. It would help if you didn't think you are right and the listener is wrong. It destroys the bridge of communication. It is usually in the form of the following:

- *Criticism and blaming.* This is when the speaker points out the other person's faults usually to show disapproval. A negative evaluation of the other person tends to make them feel bad, inadequate, unworthy, and incompetent. This reduces performance, as they feel the need to avoid you to avoid a repeat of the same.
- *Ridiculing, shaming, and name-calling.* This is language aimed at making the other person appear foolish. This type of communication is intended to make the other person share the same opinion of themselves. The listener, however, feels you are really unfair to them.
- *Diagnosing.* Sometimes one tries to

identify the reasons behind other people's behavior. Some of the statements made in diagnostic may be rude as assumptions play a significant role. We shouldn't play psychiatrists to others. It minimizes the value other people have.

Sending Solutions

Most times, we never fall short for answers when challenges arise. However, when working as a team, it is essential to give everyone else a chance of coming up with a solution. Our knowledge and experience shouldn't make us impatient with others in contributing to the team's problems. Sending answers to other people creates new problems without necessarily solving the initial challenge.

Sending solutions involves the following:

- *Ordering.* Barking commands to our employees to get things done doesn't get things done. You lose the connection to your workers, along with their respect.
- *Threatening.* This is an expression of one's intent to punish if their wishes are not

met. Pressuring your worker with consequences if they don't follow your orders doesn't make them more compliant.

- *Being the moral police.* Often we can't help ourselves but share our perspectives, thinking we know better. However, it would be best if you didn't give in to the temptation of pointing out what others should do and how they should do it.

- *Excessive/inappropriate questioning.* It's wrong to ask intriguing questions or prying questions. It would help if you didn't use questions to lead others to a conclusion or dig information out of people trying to find a solution.

- *Advising.* This is giving one's opinion about what somebody else should do or how they should behave.

Avoiding the Problem

Avoiding a bad situation isn't always the best solution for the relationship. It's true. Cooler heads get along just fine, but, if you ask me, you're still in the same situation. Finally, you'll need to address the elephant in the room.

Some communication coaches recommend a "courageous communication" training course. Some people lack the courage to speak their minds or hearts. Courageous communication assists in developing straightforward and honest communication that isn't rude and demeaning. That gives room for productive dialogue. In this case, both parties are heard as opposed to a conversation where one person only waits for a pause to respond.

Types of communication that involve avoiding problems include the following:

- *Diverting*. This is taking attention away from something as a distraction. People who do this usually change the subject or just joke as soon as they feel uncomfortable.

- *Reassuring*. This is a situation where you try to remove somebody's fears or doubts, usually by making them feel confident again. Instead of speaking what's in your mind, you decide to give affirmation. Admittedly, it is of great importance to build positive relations by assertion. However, you shouldn't use this as an excuse to avoid confronting what concerns you.

Effective communication relies on your commitment to the cause. Always research your topic to boost your confidence on the matter. Prepare for every meeting while anticipating the listener's response. You could also avoid judgy statements by losing the self-righteous act. If you are handling a problem, keep your team involved—meaning, you work together and they don't work for you.

Communication is a two-way street. Just as you would think of yourself, consider the other person. Always listen before you can be heard. If you are in a position of leadership, let your team learn from you the same way as you can learn from them. Coming up with a solution doesn't always involve your demeaning others in the process. Remember, communication affects productivity and therefore determines the success of your team.

Conclusion

Thank you for reading this book. I hope it helps you avoid emotional abuse, recover from it and nurture your social skills. The next step is to put all you have learned into practice.

Thanks a lot!

Martha McDowell

References

Abuse Defined | The National Domestic Violence Hotline. (2018). Retrieved from https://www.thehotline.org/is-this-abuse/abuse-defined/

Abuse Types and Cycle Wheel. (2013). Retrieved from http://www.ashleighspatienceproject.com/abuse-types-and-cycle-wheel.html

Desanctis, E. (2018). What Emotional Abuse Really Means. Retrieved from https://www.joinonelove.org/learn/emotional-abuse-really-means/

Hammond, C. (2018). How to Confront an Abusive Person. Retrieved from https://pro.psychcentral.com/exhausted-woman/2016/05/how-to-confront-an-abusive-person/

Law, J. (2017). Are you being emotionally abused? Take this quiz to find out. Retrieved from https://interact.support/are-you-being-emotionally-abused/

Mathews, A. (2016). When Is It Emotional Abuse?. Retrieved from https://www.psychologytoday.com/us/blog/traversing-the-inner-terrain/201609/when-is-it-emotional-abuse

Patricelli, K. (2018). Types of Abuse. Retrieved from https://www.mentalhelp.net/articles/types-of-abuse/

Safety Planning | Loveisrespect.org. (2018). Retrieved from https://www.loveisrespect.org/for-yourself/safety-planning/

What is Gaslighting? | The National Domestic Violence Hotline. (2014). Retrieved from https://www.thehotline.org/2014/05/29/what-is-gaslighting/

The Self Worth Quiz. (2019). Retrieved from https://wire.wisc.edu/quizzesnmore/SelfWorthQuiz.aspx

www.ingramcontent.com/pod-product-compliance
Lightning Source LLC
LaVergne TN
LVHW091418190726
843491LV00006B/1482